Praise for

# Sky Full of Stars

"Meg Apperson knows what it means to suffer—and yet she also knows what it means to find a way to the place of peace amidst suffering. That is what marks this book out as special. Through these powerful pages, Meg helps us see the heart, wisdom, and economy of God at work, even in the toughest moments of our lives. This hope-filled book is going to help many people—including you!"
—Matt Redman
    Grammy Award–winning songwriter and worship leader

"Meg's story uncovers the delicate layers of pain found while living and brings forth a sense of purpose that sits right alongside this pain. In telling the journey of her medically complex daughter, Avery, and weaving her past traumas within her current realities, Meg grapples with using her voice, letting go of control, and trusting outside of herself to come through these difficult days again and again. Ultimately, in *Sky Full of Stars*, Meg Apperson overcomes the wrestling in her spirit by the steady strength she finds in God and her resolve to trust in Him anyway."
—Laesa Faith Kim
    Author of *Can't Breathe*

"Having navigated my own years of heartbreak relative to losing a child and infertility, I find on the pages of Meg's book a deep soul filled with revelation, wisdom, and comfort all wrapped into one work of art. Her honest and transparent stories have something for everyone when life is complicated and questions abound. This is a read-it and share-it-with-others gift to the world!"
—Lynette Lewis
    TEDx speaker, author of *Climbing the Ladder in Stilettos*, and pastor's wife

"In her book, *Sky Full of Stars*, Meg Apperson shares with you her journey of recognizing the light even as darkness is all around. A story of letting go of dreams and embracing hope and healing that any mom who has a child with differences can understand."
—Michelle Sullivan
Author of *Eli, Included*

"Meg Apperson shares her truth—her life. It's raw. It's vulnerable. It's powerful. A must-read for any healthcare professional, advocate, or human being walking through hardship. This story of hope will revitalize your faith and open your heart to seek goodness in the depths of darkness. As an occupational therapist, Meg's words are a graceful reminder that we may never know, to the fullest extent, our clients' pain and suffering. As an inclusion advocate, Meg's words set my soul on fire in pursuit of a more inclusive world. As a children's book author, Meg's words empower me to represent children who are underrepresented. As a human being who has suffered with Panic Disorder, Anxiety, and self-worth, Meg's truth reminds me of God's goodness and that even in the deepest valleys there is light, He is steady, and I am strong. Meg, Avery, their family, and this book are a gift to the world—may it be read by many."
—Dr. Nicole Julia, OTD, OTR/L
Author of *The Able Fables*

"I already felt a part of Meg's journey by following her online. But now she's pulled back the curtain of her life in an even more profound way. Her vulnerability has been and is one of the greatest inspirations to my own online voice. The beautiful human that God has made Avery and everyone in her family to be glows through every inch of what Meg shares. I feel Meg and I are lifelong friends from reading her book. I cried out lies of perfection through the pages, pain I'd been holding on to in my own story. Her book is a safe place to feel understood. God is healing places in my heart through Meg's words. A reminder that my messy life is also beautifully laced in God's grace, just as Meg's, just as Avery's. Even as war wages around us, she reminds us that we are not an accident, but chosen and loved by God. She shows the intricate way God's love has wrapped around her family, and I believe it will give hope to all her readers.

"In this time of pain, confusion, hurt, and unknown for so many in our world, I believe this book is not only timely, but a way people will see their darkest nights are lit up by God's love. A way to know 'our pain isn't punishment, but preparation.' A way for all of us to trust God in all of life's hills and valleys. Hope that God's redemption is real and for all of us."
  —Stefanie Rouse, MMFT
    Founder of Cultivate Relationship Ministry, Christian speaker, and lifestyle, faith, and travel blogger

"We are told in Scripture that 'We must go through many troubles to enter the Kingdom of God.' We often wish this truth away, but Meg Apperson brings us home to it again. Thank God she does. The story she has to tell in this book is raw and unapologetic, yet it reveals the God who is always there—just on the other side of our agonies."
  —Stephen Mansfield
    *New York Times* bestselling author

Sky Full of Stars

# Sky Full of Stars

## Learning to Surrender to God's Perfect Plans

### Meg Apperson

SALEM
BOOKS

an imprint of Regnery Publishing

All Scriptures are taken from THE HOLY BIBLE, NEW INTERNA-
TIONAL VERSION®. Copyright © 1973, 1978, 1984, 2011 by Biblica,
Inc.™ Used by permission of Zondervan.

Salem Books™ is a trademark of Salem Communications Holding
Corporation
Regnery® is a registered trademark of Salem Communications Holding
Corporation

ISBN: 978-1-68451-063-4
eISBN: 978-1-68451-103-7

Library of Congress Control Number: 2019957978

Published in the United States by
Salem Books
An imprint of Regnery Publishing
A division of Salem Media Group
300 New Jersey Ave NW
Washington, DC 20001
www.SalemBooks.com

Manufactured in the United States of America

10 9 8 7 6 5 4 3 2 1

Books are available in quantity for promotional or premium use.
For information on discounts and terms, please visit our website:
www.Regnery.com.

# Author's Note

I feel it is my duty to remind all readers that there are always two sides to every story. I am an imperfect, partial human being—not a memory fundamentalist. I remember certain events one way, but there may be other aspects of which I am not aware that could have been added to give more scope to this book. I cannot share what I do not know.

That being said, I have tried to give as full an account of these events as possible. For the sake of fairness, in terms of poor behavior and to make this book slightly more readable, I have dropped everyone's lowest grade except my own. If you find yourself being depicted in this book in a way you do not like, please know that I do not claim to have the monopoly on redemption. I believe Jesus can make all things new—including you. And if you're wondering if I'm writing about you, then I probably am.

# The Cast

**Avery:** third child of four, one in a million, born broken, being restored, longest eyelashes in the world

**Cody:** father, generous, helpful, athletic, strongest man I know

**Macson:** oldest of four, profoundly intelligent, the reason I'm still alive

**Lolly:** really named Laura after my mom, second-born with an attitude to match her fiery red hair, most likely to rule the world

**Ryan:** youngest of four, our surprise baby who came crashing into our world when I thought my baby days were long over

**Mom/Laura/Gram:** wife to Michael, mom and home educator of eight, grandmother, ultra-marathoner, my closest friend

**Dad/Michael/Poppa:** husband to Laura, father of eight, grandfather to twenty-four (so far), Ironman athlete, Avery's favorite human on the planet

**Meg:** author of this book, recovering perfectionist, hates religion, loves Jesus and my family, cusses a little—OK, a lot

# Foreword

You're holding in your hands (or listening to) a story that has the potential to grow and expand your heart. Meg's words have the power to change your perspective and ignite a passion that will change the way you think, speak, and act. Whatever you're facing, you are brave and strong.

When my first son, David, was born with a profound disability, my world crumbled around me. My husband, Stephen, and I were told our baby would never walk or talk. He had a heart defect and only two fingers on his left hand. The dreams I had been dreaming died, and in their place, I felt a desperate sadness. Would I ever feel joy again?

As my husband and I grieved, we created a new normal, fell in love with our son—but honestly, I avoided that deep well of grief at the center of my soul. I tiptoed around the edge, terrified I would fall in. How deep was the water?

I tried to ignore the sadness. I tried to smile. I tried to think positive thoughts. I tried to focus on gratitude—but all the grief was still there, waiting to be felt.

Eventually, I dipped my toe into those dark waters. The water was deep—deeper than I expected. I did fall in. Waves of grief washed over me—but I didn't sink. To my surprise, I found I could swim.

At times I was so tired that it was hard to keep my head above water, so I would float on my back—almost numb with grief. Slowly, the water began to subside. After time I found my footing—my toes could reach the bottom. I stood up and took a deep breath. My legs were strong. I waded out of the water and dried myself off. The sun began to shine. It warmed my shoulders. Slowly, slowly, I found my way back.

I still dip my toe into those dark waters. I am not afraid of painful feelings like I was before. Even when the water is deep, I can swim. Hope is buoyant; it keeps me afloat.

Slowly, that sadness gave way to calm. I began to pivot from wishing things could be different to accepting the way they were. As much as I didn't want it, our son had a disability. This was our new life. Acceptance brought openness and opportunity. Could we find beauty in this unfamiliar place? As I opened myself up, I was surprised to see rays of light shine through the darkness. I held on to that light with everything I had.

Friend, I believe pain and grief mold and shape us in amazing ways. In an unexpected twist, God has used pain and grief to introduce me to a deeper love and a bigger joy.

Meg's story drew me in immediately. She's honest and raw. She lets us wade into grief with her and shows us how to float in deep waters. She's been through the unthinkable, and she's still here, sun on her shoulders—speaking truth and inviting us to join her.

I know you'll find yourself in Meg's story—in the midst of her pain and her bravery. You'll be encouraged on your own journey of wading through deep waters to find deeper love and bigger joy.

Lisa Leonard
Founder of Lisa Leonard Designs
Author of *Brave Love, Your Spark,* and *Be You*

# Introduction

*T*ap, tap, tap.

    I opened my eyes. *Please let that knock have been part of my dream.*
*Tap, tap, tap* again.

    *Dangit. Maybe it's Macson, and his legs are hurting again? Maybe*
*it's Bea, and she needs more suction catheters? Please let it be that.*
*Lord, you know I'm so tired. Please just heal Avery already.*

    Most of Avery's medical supplies were stored in the closet of our
master bathroom. I had taught myself to calculate exactly what we
needed to order from the supply company each month to avoid having
every closet in the house bursting at the seams with spare trachs,
catheters, and enteral feeding-tube supplies. The closet was under
control so it would be easy to find exactly what our night nurse, Bea,
might need for our eleven-month-old daughter.

    *Please let it be that,* I thought again.

    I checked my phone. Two o'clock on a cold February morning in
2016. Half-sighing, half-groaning, I rolled out of bed, groping about
in the dark for a pair of sweatpants, still hoping the knocker would be

my oldest son needing me to help him address growing-pain issues. I cracked the door open a few inches.

"She's crying inconsolably, and her heart rate is over 200. You need to come now," said the figure in the dark hallway. Bea's voice was firm and begged no question. I followed her to the living room at the front of our ranch-style home. The long, rectangular space sat adjacent to the kitchen. A change in the style of flooring signified where the kitchen ceased and our living room, which had been turned into a combination of hospital triage unit and the bedroom of our youngest child, began. What had once been a simple room decorated minimally and neutrally was now a messy, mismatched nursery boasting a cacophony of noises from various medical devices meant to sustain a struggling life and the glow of numbers from a machine that tracked the pulse and oxygen saturation of my newest baby.

Bea led the way to Avery's crib in the far corner while I shuffled along behind her, running the potential causes of tachycardia (elevated heart rate) through my head. At this time of night, the space would usually be dark, but now the room buzzed with stark lights and blaring alarms. I could hear Avery's trach-muffled screams as I drew nearer. She was four days post-op, so I wasn't surprised that she would be cranky and restless through the night, but the high heart rate was slightly more concerning. Her pulse-ox monitor read 204.

*Yeah, something is not right. God, please have mercy. OK, first things first.*

I checked Avery's soft spot. On the average child, this indention would usually be found in the middle of the top of the head, a slight depression under which the pulsing dura—the thick, membranous tissue that encases the brain and spinal cord—could be felt. But on Avery, my hand slid to the side of her head. Her unique head shape and chunks of missing skull, removed during various surgeries, allowed for easy access to pockets of gray matter, which helped me to evaluate the level of pressure on her brain. On multiple occasions, I had seen the horrifying effects of cerebral spinal fluid pooling in her ventricles as she slipped into a coma, but we'll get to that later.

I rested my fingers on her temples. I felt the pulsing and assessed whether the dura felt taut.

*Still soft. Thank God. So, not hydrocephalus. That's good.*

I rubbed my eyes. "OK, tell me about her night," I murmured softly, cradling Avery's head in my hands, checking the newly acquired zipper incision the length of my palm that spanned the back of her head and neck. Days earlier, her neurosurgeon had removed a section of her skull and pieces of vertebrae that had been compressing her brainstem. The part of her body that regulates her heart and respiratory rates, blood pressure, swallowing, and oh-so-many other functions now lay covered by mere muscles and layers of skin, relying on sutures for coverage and protection.

I learned that Avery had forcefully vomited several times during Bea's shift and had been restless. She was afebrile, meaning she did not have a fever or need supplemental oxygen.

*All good signs, minus the vomit.*

I mused for a moment, connecting the pieces of the "symptom puzzle" as I did every day—as I had been doing for close to a year.

*She's been vomiting. No sign of hydrocephalus. No obvious viral cause. Repeated episodes of vomiting can cause dehydration. Dehydration causes tachycardia. That would be easy enough. It would save me a drive to the children's hospital, and God knows I'm not driving this baby for an hour and a half with a heart rate like that.*

Serendipitously, I was born, raised, and still reside in a small town just outside the largest military base in the world. Our home sits a mere one hundred miles from a major children's hospital and craniofacial center, an incredible gift to a family like mine that commuted several times a week with our medically fragile baby to the only surgeons in the area equipped for the complexity of Avery's case.

Since time is always of the essence, I quickly decided that an infusion of IV fluids was a good first effort, and very likely a cure, if Avery was merely suffering from slight dehydration. This could be administered by our local hospital. If I could find no satisfaction there, I could always insist that she be flown to the children's hospital.

That assurance gave me some comfort. Once tucked into her car seat and solely under my care, Avery did calm slightly, though her heart rate still soared.

At our local hospital, thanks to Avery's physical appearance and trached airway, we were immediately taken to a room and assessed. Having had several run-ins with this staff before, the attending physician came to me directly. I was thankful to skip the normal middle-man resident who would fumble over his words and try to hide the fact that he had absolutely no clue where to start with Avery. After too many experiences with people too newly out of medical school to be of much help, to this day, I immediately ask for the most senior, seasoned doctor on the floor wherever I go. Luckily, most professionals who are ill-equipped identify themselves as such by excusing themselves almost as soon as they meet Avery, then lurking in the back of the room to listen and learn. She is a fascinating teaching case.

We exchanged curt greetings, and I plunged in, giving the attending physician a rundown of Avery's medical history and the last seventy-two hours. We had been seen in the emergency room at the children's hospital two days earlier for an aggressively draining seroma—a collection of clear, serous fluid that had formed at the incision site on the back of Avery's neck following her decompression surgery. The fluid had been drained, and an on-call neurosurgeon had added more stitches to the incision. The attending physician listened thoughtfully until I reached the end of my speech.

"So, how can *I* help you?" he asked hesitantly. I could see him running through the mental gymnastics of how he could treat a baby like this in such a limited facility. I told him that a complete blood count (CBC), chest X-ray, and some IV fluids would be a great help. I wanted to rule out any simple causes for her symptoms before I began chasing the big ones. His team did exactly what I asked.

Avery's heart rate trended down after the fluid, though it didn't return to her normal range. Her white blood cell count (WBC)—the number of immune system cells involved in protecting the body from infectious diseases and foreign invaders—came back at nineteen, which concerned me, but the attending physician felt confident that the number was elevated due to a stress response. The bonus of having Avery's blood drawn so frequently is that I'm very familiar with what certain numbers mean for her. I would accept a WBC of thirteen as a stress response, but nineteen made me a little uncomfortable. The doctor said he would defer to me if I felt strongly about it, but I was afraid to be "extra," so I let it go. After all, her chest X-ray was pristine and the fever that had suddenly appeared remained low enough to not be especially alarming (99.3 axillary). Fevers can also be linked to a stress response, so an elevated temperature that was too low to even be fully classified as a fever was not an incriminating symptom.

After the goal amount of fluids had infused into her deeply sleeping body, I was released to take Avery home. I knew she probably wasn't entirely fine, but the doctor was encouraging and hopeful, and I knew the local hospital had maxed its capacity to help her. Her heart rate did seem to be improving as well. The doctor felt assured that she was well enough and was simply experiencing a bump on the road to recovery after such a major surgery.

But Avery quickly informed me that she was not "well enough," as we were so desperately hoping she was.

Over the course of the day, her heart rate refused to drop below 180, and she was difficult to rouse in between naps. Her soft spot continued to feel soft, but lethargy is particularly damning evidence of neurological status change, so I packed her medical supplies for a second time and drove the hour and a half to the children's hospital.

Once we had been triaged, the resident in front of me stood in stark contrast to the professionals at the county hospital I had frequented earlier that day. Though freshly granted the title of "physician," he moved with confidence as Avery lay in my arms. His eyes narrowed as he examined her. There was no great exchange of words between us, as he seemed to be rushing. The last thing he did before leaving our curtained space was lift her pinky from its resting spot on my hand and give it a little squeeze.

No color change.

"I'll be right back," he said, excusing himself with a quick nod in my direction. My stomach did a little flip when he was true to his word, returning with the attending physician only moments later. She moved a little faster than he had as she did her own exam, listening to various organs. She stopped when she reached Avery's heart, pulling the stethoscope from her ears. "Is she always this color?" she asked me with obvious alarm.

I looked down and realized Avery's complexion had become markedly sallow since we had arrived.

"Umm, no? She's usually pink and happy and awake and, and—" I stopped to compose myself. I had only cried in front of two doctors during Avery's entire life, and those were not moments of which I was particularly proud. I willed myself to push down any tears that were threatening to spill and ruin my cool, stoic exterior. It had been a wild day. It had been a wild week. Skull surgery. Recovery. Three emergency department visits. Seven and a half hours of driving time. Honestly, it had been one hell of a long, wild year.

My efforts worked. No tears. I steeled myself again and switched into clinical mode. Avery lay in my arms as my daughter, but my mind treated her as a patient.

The attending repeated the pinky trick. "She's turning gray," she said, nodding, echoing what the young resident had undoubtedly reported to her after his examination. Turning to him, the attending physician said, "Start Vancomycin, Rocephin, and get me a lactate NOW," with fervor.

I knew what those antibiotics were. The heavy hitters, doubled up to cover as many infectious causes as possible. I understood what that blood test meant. I knew what they were checking for. I knew the attending physician suspected the infection lay under Avery's newest scar, and I knew we were racing the clock. The color in Avery's body continued to drain, and her oxygen levels became more unstable as her heart became increasingly inefficient at pumping oxygenated blood to her organs, necessitating a ventilator. She had begun to "circle the drain." Prior to that moment, hydrocephalus had been my greatest fear—but only because I had never come up against sepsis, a powerful, menacing malady in its own right.

I reached for my phone. I knew I would want as many pictures of Avery as possible if she didn't live to see the next morning, even if they were pictures of her dying. I was going to be prepared if this was the night my Lord and Savior called my baby home after a short life of so much suffering. Maybe death was how He would heal her. I also wanted to text my mom.

"Avery's gone over the cliff," my fingers typed out.

I pressed *send*.

# Chapter 1

*Do you trust Me?* God asked me one morning in the summer of 2014. With my Bible open, worship music in my ears, and a journal scribbled endlessly with prayers and dreams, I smiled.

*Of course, Lord.*

I had been a believer for most of my life. I had been raised by Christian parents and homeschooled. I had attended Bible college. I had always been involved in church and had participated as a member of the worship team from the age of twelve. And, not that the absence of these behaviors is necessarily proof of sainthood, but I had never smoked a cigarette or been drunk. While clearly not perfect, as you will undoubtedly discover if you keep reading, I was a relatively seasoned Christian and—after a few painful lessons and a decisive crisis of faith—was truly committed to following Jesus for the rest of my life. But now He wanted more.

*Do you trust Me?* He asked again.

"Yes. I do," I answered. I considered my dark season, several years earlier, when my life had been stripped down to a bare minimum. I had intentionally lost my marriage, most of my family, friends,

1

reputation—and as far as I was concerned at the time, any hope of a future. The one thing I had retained from that period was a beautiful, bubbly baby boy with the sweetest brown eyes and disposition. Macson had made single motherhood as easy as it could possibly be, and he was my greatest joy in life.

"OK, I trust You, but just don't touch my kids," I added with a chuckle, glancing over at my newest baby, Lolly, as she slept in her crib on the other side of my room. She was the spitting image of her daddy, Cody, who had swept Macson and me off our feet in a glorious display of love two years earlier. I stared at my baby girl, who possessed the sweetest curly red hair that shone like the sun. *Just don't touch my kids.*

Macson had turned five years old that year, and I was remarried to the love of my life, blissfully content with my two children, and a little uncomfortable with this sudden line of questioning.

"Yes, I trust you." I closed my Bible abruptly, as if to end the conversation. Little did I know that it was far from over. Over the next few weeks, I felt that I heard the Lord ask me the same question repeatedly. I answered the same way every time. "Yes, I trust You, but please don't mess with my children." I had no idea that that sentence was a contradiction. How could I fully trust Him if I didn't want Him to "mess" with my children? What did "mess" mean, anyway? Was God not trustworthy enough to know what my children needed more than I?

Because my experience of learning to trust God with my own life had involved so much loss, I subconsciously assumed that trusting the Lord with my children meant that I would lose one of them. And because I couldn't imagine a greater pain, I held on to my babies for dear life. I was their mother, after all. I was "in control." I knew what my children needed, and no one would ever hurt them. I thought that keeping them from suffering was the ultimate goal.

*Do you trust Me?* The question began to haunt me. I had been a Christian long enough to know that God is more interested in our growth than our comfort, but my need to control in order to protect my children was so fierce that I began to resent that inquisition from the Lord. C.S. Lewis put it perfectly when he said, "We are not necessarily doubting that God will do the best for us; we are wondering how painful the best will turn out to be."

I knew deep down that my answer to the question of trust was "No." Everything I felt I had lost in life were things I knew I could live without, but I believed I could never live without my children—and the idea of their pain or death was too much for me to bear.

I could not even fathom what would happen next in my life or how it would escalate over several years. I never could have predicted that the very next year I would be holding my nearly expired child in my arms, crying to the Lord that I was willing to surrender her to Him if it was her time, or that I would see two of my children connected to life support in separate intensive care units. The year 2015 was the year that God "messed" with my children.

In an excruciating display of grace, He asked me to place my greatest idols into His hands, the very things I held most dear—seemingly too precious to commit to my Savior for fear that He would allow something terrible to occur. This grace was awful, and I wish I could have learned about hope, trust, and His never-ending mercies differently, but He had a plan. In the worst pain I could imagine, the Lord was calling me to a new place—a place where I had no choice but to trust. I had no control, and the only things I could cling to were hope and faith. He wanted to ask me again, "Do you trust Me?" He wanted me to answer—simply, honestly—"Yes."

He was calling me to trust Him in all things. He wanted to show me the scope of His goodness, to glorify His name in my life like never before. He had a fire waiting for me that would refine me through its scorching, often seemingly unbearable heat to become the mother, wife, sister, daughter, and writer with a message of hope that He had destined me to become.

He was writing my story—a story of awful, beautiful, hope-filled grace. A story of surrender in all its glory and trauma. A story of learning to see His hand in everything, even in the dark.

A story of finding stars—His plans and purposes—in the darkest sky I had ever known.

# Chapter 2

"All of your labs look fine, but you're pregnant."

I stared at the emergency room doctor in disbelief before uttering a cuss word. (Sorry, Jesus.)

"I can't. I can't be," I stammered. "I already have a baby. I just had a baby. Lolly is only seven months old. I can't have another baby yet!"

He just stood there sheepishly, staring at his shoes, while I verbalized all my disbelief.

"I'm here because I just had surgery not even two weeks ago, and the doctor told me that there was absolutely no way I could be pregnant! They did a blood test and an ultrasound. I saw what looked like a baby on the screen when the ultrasound tech didn't know I was looking, but the OB doc on call told me it was a benign mass. He said it was nothing. I really *cannot* be pregnant."

The doctor shrugged. "You are. Your pregnancy hormone levels are high and rising."

The facts began to click in my head, and I repeated, "But I just had surgery . . . with drugs, anesthesia, morphine. I had a CT scan. That's radiation. And someone gave me Versed, even though no one warned me before they administered it. They said it's a class D drug! I couldn't nurse my baby for a while after I found out I was taking it because it's known to cause birth defects, and no one knows if it's safe to take while breastfeeding. They just cut into my abdomen ten days ago! Are you *sure* it's a baby? Nothing could survive all that!"

Because I was experiencing severe nausea and stomach pain, I had gone to the emergency room that day to rule out any post-operative complications following an appendectomy I had needed two weeks earlier. Everything had been "off" since I had stepped foot in that hospital.

The days before my appendectomy had been extremely painful. I was horribly sick, but—in classic "Meg" fashion—I had waited until I absolutely could not wait another minute before admitting to Cody that I needed to go to the hospital. I had already lost almost ten pounds from persistent nausea, but I had always prided myself on my ability to withstand much discomfort with little complaining.

For two days after I entered the hospital, no one could explain my symptoms. All tests and scans were inconclusive. I had a negative pregnancy test but a high white blood cell count; I had a mass in my uterus, but its origins were not discernible. And with a negative pregnancy test, the obstetrician who had been called to the emergency department to consult on my case dismissed my concerns. "There is absolutely no way you could be pregnant," he'd told me. "The ultrasound is showing a small mass, but it means nothing. It's not causing your pain."

The next test, a CT scan, was similarly of little help. The radiologist's report showed no sign of any appendix at all, but it did show one mass that looked like a viable uterine pregnancy and another that appeared to be a possible ectopic pregnancy. The entire emergency team was stumped and began discussing psychotic drugs as possible treatment, since they believed my agonizing stomach pain to be a figment of my imagination.

"When we asked you about your previous surgical history, why didn't you say that your appendix had been removed before?" one doctor grilled me.

"Because it hasn't been removed," I responded indignantly. My parents, who were taking turns sitting by my bed, corroborated my story. I had only ever had dental surgery.

I became known on the surgical floor as "App-less Apperson." The staff said that perhaps I was one of those rare people who had been born without an appendix. That is, until my scans landed on the desk of just the right surgeon. She located my appendix on the images and advised that it come out immediately.

By the time the surgeons laparoscopically entered my abdomen almost two days after I had sought treatment in the emergency room, my appendix had long been perforated, leaking infectious fluid throughout my peritoneal cavity. My appendix was removed, my abdomen was wiped clean, and I was discharged two days later.

I relayed this story to this new emergency room doctor again in an attempt to make him understand how absolutely *not* pregnant I was. I told him they must have run someone else's blood.

"It's your blood. I asked them to run it twice," he answered.

I had run out of options. I had run out of excuses. I looked him right in the eye and said, "Well then, do you think there's any way it's still alive?"

He patted my leg, saying, "You're going for an ultrasound right now. Let's find out."

My ultrasound revealed a six-week-old fetus with a strong heart-beat—but whether it could survive was another question. In the weeks that followed, I met with the surgeon who had performed the appendectomy. He acknowledged that the circumstances surrounding the surgery could certainly cause birth defects, especially early on during the first trimester, but he advised that the most likely outcome of my pregnancy would be spontaneous abortion. "If the fetus is damaged, your body will likely recognize that in the next two months or so and expel it," he said. "Were you planning this pregnancy? It's still early enough to terminate if there is a concern about birth defects."

Termination was not an option for my conscience. So I spent two months waiting for my body to get the memo that my baby wasn't viable—but that memo never arrived.

Because my pregnancy had begun so tumultuously, I assumed I would be given extra care to ensure that it progressed in a healthy way, but that was far from reality. Every red flag that arose was dismissed by each caregiver I met, and, of course, my anxiety found every red flag possible to keep me consistently worried. By my twenty-week anatomy scan of the developing baby, I had begun to assume that the ominous knowing that gnawed at my stomach, haunting my every waking moment with the knowledge that something was terribly wrong, was a sign that I was the sick one and that my budding baby girl, whom we had decided to name Avery Jane, was perfectly fine. The scan showed placenta previa—in which the placenta blocks the cervical opening—but a seemingly healthy baby, so I was scheduled for a repeat ultrasound in eight weeks and sent home with the relief that my horrible feeling might just have meant that I "might need a C-section or something." At the time, needing a C-section seemed like reason enough to feel anxious, so I began to relax a little and buy into the sentiment that I was simply being "hormonal," as the obstetricians and midwives that I met often told me.

At twenty-eight weeks, I settled in for another ultrasound with a technician in training who couldn't operate a sonogram machine any better than I (which is not at all). I no longer showed any sign of placenta previa, but I immediately zoned in on an abnormality that I noticed with Avery's skull. Her body measured at twenty-eight weeks gestation, but her head circumference measured weeks behind.

"There's something wrong with that. Do you see that? Right there. Will you measure that again?" I prompted the poor lady. She didn't see what I was talking about and could barely use the ultrasound probe, much less discern any pregnancy issues.

"If there's a problem, the radiologist will find it. I don't see anything," she said. (He didn't find it.)

By the time I met with my midwife again, I was livid. She read the vague radiology report to me with indifference before I exploded.

"This hospital has provided substandard, inept care from the minute I stepped foot inside seven months ago!" I cried, tears pouring down my face. (The entire health system that provides my family's medical care is centered around a single army hospital, where the emergency room, delivery rooms, ultrasound machines, and all obstetricians provide care in a single hospital structure.)

"Everything anyone has told me has been wrong! I know something is wrong. You didn't see those images, and apparently that radiologist doesn't know how to do his job. I want to see the specialist. I need to see a high-risk obstetrician right now."

This was the first time I had been so aggressive with a medical professional, but it would not be the last.

# Chapter 3

Several weeks later, I sat with a specialist following a 3-D ultrasound that had been administered with well-trained eyes.

"Your baby has craniosynostosis," he said. "Her skull plates are fused together. That's why her head is so small. Her body is growing at the correct rate, but her head is measuring in the third percentile."

The words hung in the air as I stared blankly ahead. This was the news that would change my life forever, yet I did not blink. It was as though frigid water poured through my veins because I felt cool and calm. There were no tears to push back or hysterical outbursts to suppress. My adrenaline worked its usual magic to sharpen my thoughts as they grappled with this foreign word that would take days of practice to spell and pronounce and yet would so radically alter the world as I knew it.

"Is she brain-dead, then?" I asked first, mulling over the biology of it all.

Craniosynostosis is a congenital birth defect that causes an infant's skull plate sutures to fuse prematurely. The sutures—fibrous connective tissues between the bones of a baby's skull—allow the bones to compress and overlap in the birth canal, as well as give the brain ample room for growth in the first two years of life during its peak development. They gradually fuse together over the first few years of life.

But not for Avery. I pictured her brain trapped in a cage of her body's own making, being crushed by its own protective skull.

"No, no," the doctor assured me, "Only one suture is closed. The brain is resilient and her body will compensate by allowing her brain and skull to grow in the direction of her other open sutures. She'll probably just need a surgery or two to correct things."

"A surgery or two" seemed very manageable. My baby was alive. Her brain was intact, as far as we could tell, and aside from a head circumference that measured in the third percentile (and twelve weeks behind the rest of her body), the remainder of Avery's anatomy was pristine—exactly how I had imagined my third child.

Since giving birth was the next imminent hurdle, and I needed to know what to do with the information I had just been given, I began to ask all the practical questions that occurred to me, such as whether I would need a C-section or if I could still give birth naturally. I wanted to know whether children with craniosynostosis were more likely to be born prematurely and if their unique skull issues presented problems during the pushing stage of labor, but the doctor couldn't tell me for sure. Craniosynostosis is not usually detected during pregnancy because third-trimester ultrasounds, when a skull deformity would be most easily discerned, are not routinely performed. The doctor told me that finding a case of craniosynostosis prenatally was so unusual that a procedure of care had not yet been clearly defined for these types of situations. The ambiguity of what to expect was possibly the worst news to me, since I craved answers—solid answers—to which I could cling. Walking into the unknown left me feeling out of control and spiraling.

The next eight weeks were a fog of tests and check-ups, research and revelations. A week after the first diagnosis, we learned that Avery's condition was slightly more complicated than originally reported after another, more invasive ultrasound showed a second fused suture parallel to the first. Perhaps it was my maternal instincts or all the medical journals I'd been feverishly absorbing day and night that told me the situation had turned very grave, though a bubbly, youthful genetic counselor earnestly argued with me to the contrary.

"Multi-suture synostosis is very much indicative of an underlying syndrome," I quoted to her, having read a similar sentence days before.

"No, no, not necessarily," she contradicted. "I can't find anything in your genetic history that would make us think your baby has a syndrome. This seems like simple craniosynostosis."

As sore and pregnant as I was, out of sheer indignation and "know-it-all-ness," I immediately sat up from my reclined position on the ultrasound examination table. "Bicoronal craniosynostosis is syndromic in 96 percent of cases. The basic statistics of this are not on my side," I responded with a hint of snap. "And most of the time, the cause is some random mutation, so my familial history has no bearing on this either. Or I could carry a mosaic gene."

I stopped. I'm not usually so forceful with strangers. And anyway, my mother was in the room with me, and I half-expected her to chide me for being rude. (She didn't.)

I started again, a little quietly, since I wasn't especially well-versed on the pronunciation of the French name that I would utter over and over in the days to come. "Crouzon, umm, syndrome." The name felt foolish to me and full of terror, as the googling of such a term ushered a slew of images too graphic for me to understand. "Characterized by bicoronal craniosynostosis, potential internal abnormalities, and no limb defects," I quoted from memory. The grainy black-and-white ultrasound images of Avery's perfect hands and feet flashed through my mind—ten perfect fingers and ten perfect toes. If she had a syndrome, it seemed most likely to me that it would be Crouzon syndrome, though none of the specialists we consulted agreed with me.

My words were a grave prophecy. Exactly two weeks before her due date and after a rather precipitous labor, Avery entered the world without a moment to spare and in a very bad state. Neither my birth team nor I had realized I had suffered a placental abruption at some point and was bleeding silently and dangerously as Avery's "lifeline" tore to shreds—a horrible complication that can easily steal the life of both mother and child.

Having opted out of an epidural for pain management so I could be in control of the pushing stage of my labor, the moments immediately after Avery's delivery were especially shaky. Although I was relieved to be finished with my task, the real trauma began as I caught the first glimpse of a more distorted head and face than I had possibly considered. She was whisked away to a side table where the neonatal intensive care (NICU) team had camped during my two-hour labor, and I listened for her cry, steeling myself for the possibility that no such cry would come.

Avery did cry out once or twice before a nurse gently approached the bed where I lay and carefully uttered the words, "Your baby is having some trouble breathing. It looks like she can't breathe out of her nose. When she cries, she is pink, but as soon as she closes her mouth, she turns blue. We're going to have to transport her to the NICU at the closest children's hospital. They have all the best specialists there who will know what to do for her. I'm sure they can just do a little surgery and open up her nose." (They couldn't.)

I nodded, still breathing with much concentration through the afterbirth pains. I knew the primary complications for syndromic craniosynostosis were airway issues, but the idea that we were a seemingly simple surgery away from a baby who could breathe and eat normally comforted me and gave me the strength to withstand the whirlwind that ensued. (Blissful ignorance, we'll call it).

A nurse laid Avery in my arms for a brief moment, and I fully realized the extent of her external anomalies. She was wrapped in a white towel, wearing a little hat the hospital provided that read, "Delivered From Above." The words had a military significance, but they also meant something special to me. Delivered from above. Sent from Heaven. Avery was God's gift to me.

He was about to use her to shake things up in a very serious way.

# Chapter 4

Avery was born at 6:30 in the evening on March 27, 2015. The pushing stage had been hard because fused skull plates cannot compress in the birth canal as they are supposed to. Avery emerged, and the doctor suctioned her mouth and nose. She gurgled for a moment and then cried once. The doctor cut her umbilical cord and handed her off to a nurse standing directly to his right. As Avery was being assessed, my doctor delivered the placenta.

Prior to giving birth, the hospital staff had given me the option to deliver at the children's hospital where Avery would be treated afterward, thinking perhaps it was more efficient to deliver at a facility that could give her more invasive care—but no one was convinced that she would actually need that level of it. After Avery had been diagnosed initially by the perinatologist via ultrasound, Cody and I had been referred to a maternal fetal medicine clinic at the clinic attached to the children's hospital to confirm the craniosynostosis. The specialists there discovered an additional fused skull suture and noted possible enlargement of one of Avery's kidneys. We were then referred to a pediatric neurosurgeon to discuss his take on the ultrasound images and talk over the best course of action for Avery after her birth. My obstetrician and the neurosurgeon both agreed there was nothing about the images that indicated any type of syndrome might complicate Avery's newborn period. They also said that I would be safe to deliver at our small hospital—a primitive facility compared to the one where we had been meeting with specialists. Everyone agreed Avery would need surgery in the months after her birth, but it seemed that we could still possibly have an average delivery and recovery there.

As it turned out, my delivery was indeed manageable there. Avery's care after birth, however, was certainly not. As the NICU team worked on my newborn at a nearby table, I lamented to my mother that I had made a terrible choice.

"I can't believe this. Now they'll have to take her in the ambulance and she'll be alone until I'm released." I shook my head in exasperation. "I should have delivered at the children's hospital. How could I have made such a stupid decision? I didn't pack for this!" Somehow, the contents of my hospital bag seemed of the utmost importance even as the entire trajectory of my life began to change and my old life burst into red, scorching flames.

My mom hugged me and reminded me there was no way anyone could have known how sick Avery would be. "You didn't know, you didn't know," she repeated. "The doctors thought this would be fine. This should have been fine. You'll recover tonight and get released tomorrow, and then we'll figure everything out. You can always go home and pack a little more."

My doctor interrupted us to ask, "Were you bleeding when you came to the hospital? Is that why you came in?" He was turning my placenta over in his hands, inspecting it closely. Parts of it looked like they had been turned inside out, but I didn't think anything of it. Honestly, I couldn't conceive of anything worse than having a baby who turned blue whenever she stopped crying.

I stopped beating myself up long enough to answer, "Uh, no, I came in because I had a couple of good contractions and because I had no idea what to expect with this labor. I didn't know if it would go too fast because her head is so small, so I just decided to risk coming too early and getting sent home."

"So, you weren't bleeding and you weren't in active labor—you just decided to come in?" he clarified.

"Yeah," I answered. "The neurosurgeon I saw after Avery was first diagnosed warned me that I might not have to dilate all the way to ten centimeters before her head came out. So I didn't want to wait until it was too late. I'm only exactly thirty-eight weeks pregnant today, but I had a feeling." I shrugged.

"You made the right call to deliver here," he said very seriously. "You had what we call a 'silent abruption.' Your placenta was tearing away, but the blood was trapped inside your uterus. If you had tried to drive all the way to the children's hospital, every tiny bump on the road would have worsened the tearing. Both you and the baby could have died in the car."

My exasperation disappeared in an instant, and my mom and I looked at each other in disbelief. If a single doctor had felt strongly that Avery should be delivered at the children's hospital, I would have listened. I would have elected to deliver an hour and a half from my home. I would have gotten into the car that afternoon after a particularly uncomfortable contraction and possibly bumped and jostled Avery and myself straight into Heaven. I knew in that moment the Lord had purposely shielded us from knowing how broken Avery truly was— because if I had known, I would have made a decision that might have cost both of us our lives.

I had been supernaturally spared. Avery had been spared. God had a purpose in all of this, and He wanted both of us alive.

This realization was the first in my collision with the truth about Avery. She wasn't a mistake flailing about in the universe. She hadn't merely "happened" to take up residence in my womb. She had been carefully crafted and sent to me. Her journey had been tumultuous but protected. War had been waged over this seemingly inconspicuous soul. While the rest of the world was unaware, the forces of Hell sought to destroy her, to thwart her crash into Earth, where she would make her mark before she had even learned to speak. When sickness and surgery should have claimed her, she clung on. When delivery complications should have stolen her, she remained. My God, the Creator of the Universe, was the Creator of Avery. He had thought of her before the beginning of the world and waited through time and space to bring her to fruition. My baby had a job to do, and nothing could stop her— though a lot of things would try in the days to come.

Dear Silly Things, never underestimate Avery.

# Chapter 5

I was not able to hold Avery again for several hours after her birth. When she had been settled into the NICU and thoroughly examined by the neonatologist on call that night, I was wheeled to her floor, where other babies who luckily required only minimal intervention lay. This hospital was not equipped to handle a child as sick as Avery. My mom pushed my wheelchair over to Avery's bed, where she lay underneath a warming lamp, covered in wires. A short white tube protruded from her lips to force her to continue breathing out of her mouth, since as soon as it closed, her face would turn dark blue. I held my baby for an hour or so until the transport team arrived, while a nurse stood behind me holding an oxygen mask very close to Avery's face.

The ambulance arrived to take Avery away, ushering in a trend of painful separation that would mark so much of her new little life. Apparently, someone thought it might be upsetting for me to see her being strapped onto a gurney while screaming bloody murder, so I kissed her goodbye, and a nurse wheeled me to the recovery floor. My parents followed close behind to make sure I was comfortable while

Cody stayed with Avery. I showered and changed into pajamas between routine checks by the nurses before I was surprised by one last visit from my baby. The medics transporting Avery to the children's hospital brought her to my room so I could see her one more time.

She was attached to the gurney, so I could not hold her. But they opened one of the clear sides of the isolette encasing her so that I could hold her hand. I snapped a few more pictures, and then she was taken away. My husband accompanied Avery on her journey to the children's hospital, and my parents returned to my home to watch my older children, six-year-old Macson and one-year-old Lolly. So I lay in the recovery room alone. The hospital staff had delivered a breast pump, since I had lofty plans to breastfeed Avery as soon as she was able, so I busied myself with pumping and researching.

I studied all of the photos I had taken of Avery, looking for a clue as to what her syndrome might turn out to be. I zoomed in on her toes. I had read that some kids with Pfeiffer syndrome (a type of craniosyn-ostosis) had broad toes. I couldn't see anything wrong with her toes, but I checked the photos again and again throughout the night to see if somehow the images had changed or if perhaps I would suddenly see them with new clarity. Was there webbing between her fingers that I was missing? Children with Apert syndrome (another serious form of craniosynostosis) often have webbing of the fingers and toes. If Avery had Pfeiffer syndrome, she might be deaf. All of the different syndromes came with an increased risk of vision loss and at least partial hearing loss. I spent the night envisioning a life with a deaf and blind baby.

I desperately needed to see her—partly because I was so distraught by the fact that my newborn was strapped inside an isolette in the back of an ambulance with no one to hold her when she cried, and partly because I needed to study every inch of her.

I needed to understand what had happened. I felt a frantic need to know what type of syndrome she had. I thought that knowing what ailed her would let me plan a neat and tidy future for her. I erroneously believed that if I knew the life expectancy and possible complications that went with her syndrome, I would be able to foresee all the issues we might encounter and never be caught off guard.

I did not realize that my quest for answers would be a source of pain for years to come. I did not know that my need to understand was a coping mechanism. I couldn't accept what I couldn't understand; I couldn't grieve what didn't make sense to me. I would slowly see how the inability to have resolution was a painful, yet important test. The inability to have Avery's diagnosis with a prim and proper explanation was about strengthening a muscle of faith. Jesus was teaching me, by way of pain and confusion, that my preferred method of coping was not His intended way. He was beginning to show me that He had always been the Source of ultimate peace I so desperately sought. I wanted to trust Him, but I also wanted control. My need to manage was limiting my ability to access that peace, so He graciously, achingly stripped that illusion from my hands. The loss of that illusion sent me spiraling right into His arms.

Before I was discharged the next morning, at the end of their shift, the nurses who cared for Avery in the small, primitive NICU brought me the most thoughtful gifts. Three people quietly knocked on my door and presented me with her belongings, such as the hat she had worn directly after delivery, the identification band that had been attached to her ankle, and a paper on which they had taken impressions of her tiny feet. I was stunned at how thoughtful and kind they were. These people had been up all night, and instead of rushing home to get on with their lives, they had made an extra trip to visit the room of a mother with empty arms.

If that isn't goodness, I don't know what is.

# Chapter 6

My newborn and I had already been separated for a night when I raced to her side on the fourth floor of the specially equipped children's hospital. She lay, silent and sleeping, in the far left corner of the NICU pod. Sunlight streamed in from a nearby wall of windows and lit her crib, a spotlight on the child I was eager to see. Avery's bed was the only crib in the pod that saw direct sunlight at various times during the day. It was glorious to feel the warmth of the sun and see its amber glow in a world that now felt so dark and unknown, cold and sterile.

I stood next to her bed for a long time and simply stared at her. It was almost instinctual to take a few moments of silence and stillness in this foreign place. I gathered my thoughts and tried to piece together the scene before me. I would decide how to feel after I had acquired the facts. There were wires and sensors and screens displaying foreign numbers. Sharp lines danced in rhythmic waves. There were parents sitting beside other beds, and in the distance, I could hear the sniffling that results from recently shed tears. I steadied myself before glancing up at the overly cheerful, though incredibly helpful nurse. She looked as though she had a lot to tell me, but she exercised significant restraint as I eased myself into my new role.

"Can I hold her?" I asked quietly.

*This is nonsense. I can't wait to get her out of here. God, You're going to fix this for me, right? You could make Yourself look really good if You'd just heal her, like, today.*

It seems almost comical to me now. The idea of managing God. Suggesting ways to intervene as though He needed my help in improving His image.

Asking the nurse that question rattled me. It put me in my place as the visitor in the room and marked the moment that everything I knew about motherhood changed. I could not hold my own child without checking first to see if it was safe. I could not pick her up without assistance, since she lay tangled in a sea of cords and sensors connected to machines that I did not yet understand.

"Of course!" the nurse answered. Her volume matched mine and her confidence calmed my nerves a bit. Her experienced hands navigated the web of machinery quickly as she lifted Avery out of her bed and set her in my arms.

I had removed my outer layer of clothing so that a slim white nursing tank top was all that lay between Avery and my skin. I had always heard that "skin to skin" contact with newborns was important, so I rested her head up under my bare neck and held her still for a while.

"That's good," the nurse told me, "She knows her mama, so that will make her feel safe. She can smell you."

Without looking up, I said, "Yes, well, her nose is blocked with bone, so she probably can't smell anything."

"Oh..." The nurse trailed off for a second before adding, "Well, she can hear your heartbeat."

"Kids like this usually have hearing loss too, so it's possible that she's deaf."

"Well... soon she'll be able to recognize your face."

"She might not be able to see because of the way her eyes sit in her head, so she could be deaf, blind, and unable to smell."

I was aware that the words I uttered did not match my face as I finished situating Avery on my chest, and I finally looked up at the nurse blankly. There was no emotion in my voice. My face was neutral. It was as though I wanted her to know that I was not afraid of the truth—I would not shy away from the possibility of the worst-case scenario. I was almost expecting it. I would do everything in my power to be prepared for it. The nurse stopped trying to cheer me up, but she still smiled. She didn't seem fazed by my militant realism. I expected she had seen lots of mothers like me. During our stay, she handled me with delicate, nuanced gloves that didn't make me feel handled at all. I imagine my grief made me seem unpredictable, but her experience and unwavering softness guided me toward confidence, little by little.

Everything about this place was foreign. The protective beds and the children with translucent skin were new to me. Occasionally, I would be startled by the sudden emergence of a limb poking up from the bottom of an incubator. The inhabitant had escaped my notice for several days because of its shockingly small size and, even more sadly, lack of visitors. One would have to stand directly next to the incubator and look straight down to see the baby with visible veins that could have easily fit in the palm of my hand.

I came to know my own child in this sea of sadness. Newborns came and went during our time there. One, the daughter of a junkie prostitute, came with an extra finger and a terrible shake, which I now know to be withdrawal. Her biological mother met and held her once, before signing the papers to relinquish all her maternal rights. She said she had other children at home. She did not need another. The baby was named Grace by the adoptive parents who came to take her several days later. This was one rare happy ending.

Another baby had been born prematurely but had completed his many months in the NICU and was waiting for discharge. The hospital staff was having trouble locating his mother. She wasn't ready for him, she said when they finally reached her. I learned that she had been saying this for over a month. I never saw her once.

Molly was also born prematurely, but she had been holding steady. She was showing signs of an impending colon perforation—which is common among premature babies because they are not designed to interact with the world just yet—but it could not be treated until it became absolutely necessary.

Carson's parents were learning to empty his colostomy bag when we met. I do not know what happened to Carson, but I do remember passing his mother months later when Avery was in the ICU on a separate floor. Carson's mother did not notice me in the elevator because she was weeping and frantically pressing the elevator buttons. She pushed "4", which meant that Carson was still in the NICU. He had not graduated as Avery and some of the others had.

Gavin made me cry more than once. He was operated on repeatedly in our room of incubators. He was too fragile to survive a trip to an operating theater, so all of the mothers were asked to step into the hallway while scrubs, caps, and masks were donned and the immediate area where our babies lay was sterilized. One night, Gavin's mother arrived too late to see him before he passed. He had not survived the operation. I stood outside the glass doors and wept as his mother wailed. It was all too much.

Up until that point, the NICU was the saddest, darkest place I had ever been. It was our introduction, a not-so-gentle teacher in this new world of pain and loss and parents whose cries flooded the hallways. I did not know then that things could be so much worse.

Motherhood had indeed changed forever. I could no longer mother in my own strength because I had none. Each of my children, in both sickness and in health, needed a new mother—one who must desperately rely on her God, the ultimate and original Mother and Father.

# Chapter 7

I've been writing since I was a little girl, so blogging was not much of a stretch for me. I've always loved words. Reading came easily before I turned five years old. By the time I was ten, I had filled notebook after notebook with fictional stories. I was a deep feeler and thinker, so my stories involved plots that were far beyond my age (who writes about heartbreaking divorces in elementary school?) and were always full of pain, loss, and love. I felt positive, at the wise old age of eight, that writing could not actually be a lucrative job, so it never made my "Future Career" list (I literally made a list at nine years old so I could actively pursue the right profession as early as possible). But I still enjoyed it immensely.

I didn't write much, other than essays and papers in high school and college, so I became rusty and forgot my old hobby. It wasn't until I discovered lifestyle blogs, about five years or so behind everyone else, that I considered writing again. I was a single mother at the time and barely had the freedom to eat regular meals, much less write for pleasure, but a seed had been planted in my heart. After Cody and I married, I purchased my first domain, FourFineLives.com. I was thrilled, and for the first six months, I posted absolute drivel. I posted my silly opinions as though the world needed to hear them, recipes, our pregnancy announcement, Avery's gender and name, and other miscellaneous frivolity.

When we received Avery's diagnosis, I didn't plan to share what we were facing with anyone except our immediate family. I withheld the news for weeks before reluctantly sharing it with my friends on social media (my "following" consisted of only friends and family at that point). The information already had been gradually leaked, so I knew I needed to speak out and let everyone to know that we were fine, but we would love their prayers and support.

Because the only proof of defects came from fuzzy ultrasound images, there was much we didn't know about Avery's condition before she was born, and I spent about six weeks in feverish research. Blogs chronicling a family's journey with craniosynostosis were so rare and often so depressing that the research left me with more anxiety than comfort. And I knew that Avery's condition was more complex than most because she had multiple fused sutures—so even fewer blogs felt relatable.

I knew syndromic craniosynostosis was accompanied by airway issues, feeding difficulties, and a lot of need for medical intervention, but that's where the information stopped. Were children with craniosynostosis syndromes able to breastfeed? Were their deliveries normal? How long did they stay in the NICU after birth? How did siblings fit into the mix? Did everyone in the family need genetic testing? What were the cranial reconstructions like?

The ambiguity of what we were possibly facing was so overwhelming that I had little hope for anything other than a miracle. I needed a miracle, and if I didn't get one, I didn't know how I would face what might come next. The unanswered questions and feelings of helplessness were the darkest tunnel in the prenatal period.

After Avery was born, I still wasn't sure how I felt about sharing the extent of her condition with friends. The night of her birth, she was whisked away to the children's hospital, and I was left to recover alone in my hospital room an hour and a half away. I had snapped so many pictures of Avery before she was taken, but the only one I could bring myself to post of her to announce her arrival was a photo of her empty "going home" outfit mocking me from my hospital bag. My baby would not be going home. My arms were empty. It felt like a cruel joke to arrive at the hospital with a baby tucked safely inside my stomach and leave with nothing.

When we were reunited the next day, as I held her tiny body and severely deformed head, two roads clearly presented themselves before me: shame or pride.

The nurses shielded the other visitors in our NICU pod from Avery's appearance, and the doctors spoke in hushed tones when they used words like "abnormal" and "defective." When the other parents of the infants in our room caught sight of her, they stared and then looked away, refusing to look me in the eye. Cody even asked me to consider not sharing any pictures of Avery on social media to avoid upsetting any sensitive Facebook friends and family with her jarring appearance. *Will I hide my daughter? Will I be ashamed that her features aren't conventional? Who the hell cares about "conventional" anyway? Will I be hurt and upset by the stares? Will I let others' reactions to my child dictate how I live my life?*

Anger and indignation rose in my heart. I was overwhelmingly proud of Avery's fighting spirit and repulsed by the thought of her feeling ashamed of herself, as I had been for most of my life. I was incensed by the suggestion that the way Avery looked dictated the kind of life she could lead. I didn't care if people found her hard to see. They could look away. I knew everything about Avery's life was going to be bold and brave; she had already shown me that in the first twenty-four hours of her life. I wouldn't let anyone hide her because she was different. She didn't need anyone to approve of her to make her worthy. She was born worthy.

I posted her first picture. I wanted to tell her story. I wanted the world to really see Avery in all her humanity. I wanted everyone to see that people with physical differences are not scary. I wanted the world to see her power, her will to survive. And I wanted to tell our story for the next mom who heard the words, "Your baby has craniosynostosis." I wanted to be there on her screen when she googled the terms that scared her to death and made her sick to her stomach so that she would know she will never be alone. I wanted to write so that she could find us, so that she could see that things were going to be OK, so that she might find hope.

I believed God was smiling at the decision. I had no idea the extent of the story He was weaving, but I knew He wanted me to tell it, whatever it was. He made me a writer. A sensitive, philosophical seeker with a magnet for pain and a knack for telling stories with the click of the keys on my laptop.

I was once a reluctant advocate, but God's purpose for Avery has been impressed on my heart so strongly that I'm compelled to share His work in our lives. I'm compelled to share how He takes "broken" and turns it into "beautiful"—how even in the darkness, He has a plan for all our pain.

# Chapter 8

Avery was not blind or deaf, which we learned in the first few weeks following her birth. Cody and I were immediately relieved, but naively so, since there was still so much of her condition that remained a mystery to us. Still, the knowledge that I might be able to verbally communicate with her one day was a great comfort.

Then came the appointment I had been waiting for: the genetics department was called in for a consultation. All the questions I had been asking for eight prenatal weeks hung in the air as the geneticist quietly assessed Avery's features. We were told that her genes and the doctors who specialized in unlocking their secrets would hold the key to Avery's treatment. I had been promised answers, and, while I knew the answers I might receive could break my heart, I believed that this soft-spoken, gray-haired woman in muted colors possessed them all. The specialist took measurements and closely inspected Avery's fingers and toes. She extended and retracted my baby's limbs and closely studied her ears, commenting on their "low-set" appearance.

I had no idea how many clues into a child's health are scattered all over their exterior. Palm creases and the spaces between toes told stories that I had never considered. The height of ears gave an indication of what lay underneath the flesh.

"Your baby has Crouzon syndrome," the geneticist said, after several minutes of quiet.

"That's what I have been thinking. That's what I've been calling it for the last couple of months, anyway," I responded, desperate for her to know that she could speak freely and specifically with me. I had been studying the human genes specific to craniosynostosis syndromes for eight weeks. I knew the name of the likely mutated gene and the exons that probably housed the supposed mutation. I knew that Crouzon syndrome could result from the mutation of three different genes, and that the responsible gene dictated how severe the clinical manifestation of the syndrome would be. We began to discuss the implications of fibroblast growth factor receptor (FGFR) 2 or 3 and how a mutation of 2 was the most likely scenario.

She asked me if I had experience in the field of genetics, and I laughed. "Only Google School of Medicine," I told her.

"Well, I'm impressed," she said, smiling warmly.

That was all the affirmation I needed to continue my compulsive research. If I was going to be the mom of a child with a genetic mutation, I was going to be the best, most competent mother there was. (That idea seems laughable now, as though there is some type of Special-Needs Mom competition.) But the geneticist had given me a gift. I felt confident in my competence and began to believe that despite my lack of training and education, nothing about Avery's diagnosis or care was beyond me. A seed was planted that day that grew steadily into a level of self-assurance I had never experienced. I felt powerful.

For years, my power had been stolen from me—and sometimes I'd given it away—but in the NICU at the children's hospital, I was beginning to reclaim it. God had made me Avery's mother. No matter what happened, He would give me all the tools I needed to support her. I knew it would hurt, but I also knew I could do it.

Our appointment lasted for a long time. Finally, the geneticist hit me with the sentence that I knew was coming—even though I could never be completely prepared for it, despite my best efforts.

"Crouzon syndrome frequently presents with various internal abnormalities, so she may have defects that we haven't found yet."

My heart sank with knowing.

*God, please, please, please. Let Avery be different.*

She wasn't. The next two days confirmed all my prenatal fears. Additional testing showed that Avery's anatomy was full of surprises. She had a heart defect, kidney defect, excess fluid in the ventricles around her brain, and choanal stenosis, which is a narrowing of the nasal passages. In Avery's case, the narrowing was so significant that she was barely able to move air through her nose. This was the condition responsible for her unsteady upper airway. We did not yet know that Avery's skull hid one more surprise known as "Chiari malformation," but we'll get to that.

The mystery of Avery's anatomy, the puzzle I had been so desperate to solve, seemed to finally reveal itself—and the truth both comforted and terrified me. I had answers, some of them anyway, and yet there was still so much "wait and see." The geneticist had given Avery an unofficial diagnosis, but we still had to wait for the official word from her blood tests. At that time, no one had thought to tell me that sometimes blood tests don't provide all the answers to genetic questions. Our genes can be too complex.

I fell asleep most nights praying, begging for my baby's healing. For over a year, I felt that God's answer to my pleading was "no." But, in fact, I would one day see that what I interpreted as a "no" was actually a "yes."

*Yes, Meg. This story will be about great healing—My way and in My time. Trust Me.*

This answer deeply frustrated me at the time. As a Christian, I knew I should be content in all things. Trusting Christ. Repeating the verse about God working all things together for the good of those who love Him (Romans 8:28) ad nauseam. But I was angry, and I couldn't pretend not to be. I wanted Avery's healing, and I wanted it immediately. I was ready to trust as long as God operated on my timeline.

This anger separated me from grieving with my husband, who chided me for my rage, reminding me of the all-powerful God who could strike me with lightning for being so disrespectful, so full of questions. I learned that none of us grieve the same way at the same time, even when we are grieving the same thing. I wanted us to have a shared experience of grief, but now I see that the idea is largely impossible. We have to give each other space for our own experiences, our own journeys. My husband and I followed the same God, but in our own unique ways.

What I saw in those days demanded questions and answers, and I knew that my God had never chided me for asking Him the hard questions. I felt Him say once in the midst of my wrestling, *I can handle your anger. I'm not offended. I can handle your questions.*

My God wasn't striking His grieving children for grappling with pain. He knew pain. He had watched His own Son suffer once. He didn't blame me for my anger. He knew I was only human, so He let me grapple. And grapple I did.

Cody just grappled more respectfully and with fewer questions, apparently.

# Chapter 9

Our time in the neonatal intensive care unit was both exhausting and mind-numbingly repetitive.

Every day, I would wake up at seven in the morning after a night of getting up to pump breastmilk every two hours. I would get ready and head to the hospital, hoping to catch morning rounds. I would stop by the Starbucks in the hospital lobby for a coffee—my daily Americano. I would wait at the elevator with my scalding cup. I would wish that the hospital had stairs because I did not enjoy waiting for the elevator. Waiting felt inefficient, and I needed something to do with my restlessness. I would switch my coffee cup between hands when the heat seeped through the sleeve. I would catch morning rounds and hear the same information about Avery, day after day. I would hold my baby and chat with the nurse who had been caring for her. I would pump again, then hold Avery again.

Then it would be time for lunch. I would eat in the hospital cafeteria, sometimes with my mom (who spent weeks with me), sometimes alone, perusing medical journals. I would spend the rest of the afternoon alternating between pumping breastmilk (excessively, but I'll tell you about the source of that compulsion later) and holding Avery. After dark, I would leave for dinner and return to my room at the Ronald McDonald House, a charity that allows families to stay near their hospitalized children as long as necessary for a subsidized fee. I would pump once again before bed and then pass out.

My routine kept me sane and allowed me to operate on a hazy "autopilot." I tried to appreciate things outside my circumstances, like how spring had officially "sprung" and how beautifully the trees outside the hospital were blooming in shades of pink and pearly whites, but it was hard to think about anything outside of my routine, and my brain was utterly packed full of new medical information. I kept a small journal scribbled with sketches of brains, kidneys, and hearts—diagrams to help me better understand the function of normal human anatomy and how Avery's differed—as well as medical terminology to look up and questions to remember to ask during the next morning's rounds. I had a lot on my mind.

Avery had been in the NICU for twelve days, eating through a small orange tube inserted down her throat into her stomach. We had been trying oral feeding with the help of a therapist—but babies are nose breathers by design, and sucking, swallowing, and breathing without two functional nasal passages proved too difficult for Avery. We did not know then that she also had a serious brain defect that would have complicated her ability to eat, regardless of her nasal passages.

The attending physician responsible for Avery's care approached me gingerly about a surgical procedure to help her get adequate nutrition. He recommended giving Avery a gastrostomy tube—a small, external button attached to a device that connects the stomach to the abdominal wall in order to easily supply the patient with nutrition.

I knew that a permanent feeding tube was necessary, but the psychological pain of signing the consent for such a procedure and Avery's first sedation made me feel as though I was failing her as a mother.

*It's a silly feeding tube. Get yourself together, woman. She'll go through much worse before this is over.*

The surgery was simple and routine, performed commonly on all types of children (and even adults). It was a straightforward procedure, but my agreeing to the first scalpel that would slice into my baby's perfect skin felt like a betrayal. I felt like I was signing off on her "defects," as though autographing the necessary form was my agreement that she was horribly broken, as though I was siding against her anatomy with those who would classify her as defective and abnormal. As her mother, my signature was my agreement to cause her pain—and if something went wrong, it would be my fault.

Another issue on the table was the fact that once Avery was intubated, she might not be able to be extubated. Her airway situation was already tenuous. She was a newborn baby who was already having to learn to breathe in a way that was contrary to her nature and anatomy. The concern was that intubating her might cause swelling in her trachea or confuse her brain to the extent that she might not be able to breathe without the help of a ventilator. Any procedure at this stage was risky, and I was signing the form that might begin a cascade of complications.

*Oh, God—open her nose tonight. Please. Don't let her go through this. It's going to cause her so much pain.*

Of course He knew that. He knew about the pain, and He allowed it. In fact, He was counting on it. My own pain induced an obsession with collecting information and finding fault. If the surgery went poorly, it would be my fault since I had allowed the operation.

Avery's genetic results came back, and we learned that the initial Crouzon test was negative. This meant that we needed to take another sample to send for even more invasive testing. Most Crouzon cases are caused by a mutation in the FGFR 2 gene, but Avery's mutation could not be found.

I knew that she was rare, but the results of the test put Avery into a different category entirely. She wasn't just "rare"—she was extraordinary.

I had put so much hope in having a clean Crouzon diagnosis that learning the situation with Avery's genes was even more complex sent me further into the data. I desperately sought the "faulty" gene that had caused her syndrome. In fact, during that first year, we were to discover that no genetic mutation could be found in Avery. Her chromosomes were all normal and appropriately placed. She did not have Crouzon syndrome and tested negative for all the two hundred known craniosynostosis syndromes. The fault went unfound, and yet I did not stop searching. I desperately needed to know why this had happened or who had caused it—or at the very least, just *why*. My mind was occupied with this question during every waking moment for Avery's first two years of life.

I would later learn that no "why" will change what is. I may never know why or what caused Avery's condition, and knowing will not heal her. Knowing will not take away the pain. I can only focus on Who holds the keys to life and death. Jesus is enough. Whether Avery lives or dies, whether I go to my grave with whys unknown, Jesus must be enough.

# Chapter 10

When Avery was two weeks old, a doctor sliced through her skin with a scalpel for the first time. It was a stressful morning. The nurse caring for her was not her usual primary nurse; she was being shadowed by a nurse in training, and neither seemed very comfortable with Avery.

For one thing, the IV in Avery's hand had "blown." I pointed this out to one of the nurses, who simply tapped her finger across Avery's increasingly swollen hand and mumbled something noncommittal. Some of the plastic hardware attached to the IV was beginning to dig into Avery's knuckle and slice open her water-logged tissues, but the area did not bleed. I mentioned the IV several more times, but felt too new at the "medical mother" role to make any real noise.

In addition to the obvious stress of sending my newborn into surgery, Avery's main nurse seemed very annoyed by the fact that Avery would not stop screaming. My husband and I were horrified to find her holding a pacifier inside Avery's mouth as our baby frantically swung her head from side to side, arching away from the nurse.

"Oh my GOD, you can't put a pacifier in her mouth!" I rushed toward her. "Avery's nose is blocked with bone. She can't breathe with a pacifier in her mouth! You're suffocating her!" I grabbed Avery and attempted to console her, but there was nothing to do in those days to console her. Cody was red with anger, and we were both stunned by the nonchalant response we received.

"Oh," the nurse said flippantly, "that's why we couldn't get her to latch on to the thing." She and the nurse in training shrugged their shoulders and walked out. Cody and I looked at each other in disbelief.

The anesthesiologist came to take Avery to surgery and announced that we were going to need a new IV because the one in her hand was badly blown. I could barely contain my anger when I told him I had been pointing this out to the nurses, who didn't seem to care or really have any idea what to do. The anesthesiologist removed the IV, exposing the cut that had resulted from her water-logged skin's swelling to the point of easily slicing open against the plastic IV port. A chunk of her skin flapped open, exposing a gaping white wound.

I had thought that Avery's G-tube surgery would result in her first scar, but I was wrong. Five years later, her first scar is a half-inch-long white line across the third knuckle on her left hand, the result of poor care and my inability to advocate for her the way she needed me to. It was the last time I'd ever let something hurt Avery so needlessly. The next time one of her IVs "blew," I told the nurse it was compromised and that she could remove it immediately or I would remove it myself. It was an aggressive stance to take, but Avery never received another senseless scar. And I was never wrong about an IV.

We sat in the NICU's waiting area two floors above the surgical wing. Avery's ENT (Ear, Nose, and Throat) doctor had taken the opportunity to look through her nasal passages with a scope while she was already under anesthesia for the gastrostomy procedure, so we were there for several hours. I was dreading the news. Something in me expected the worst. A week before, in a single afternoon, we had learned of Avery's internal anomalies—including heart and kidney defects and water on her brain—and ever since, I had felt sure that all the news would be downhill from there. I was both right and a little wrong.

Our first piece of news was bad. The ENT had scoped Avery's nose as soon as she was under anesthesia and came to tell us that her nasal passages were so small that even their smallest scope had been unable to make it through. She said we would repeat the procedure in the future, but our only hope for improvement would be Avery's physical growth. I asked if there was a surgery to open small nasal passages, but there wasn't. We would have to wait and see.

After that news, I fully expected that Avery would come out of surgery on a ventilator, too confused or swollen to be able to breathe solely through her mouth as she had been, but I was wrong. She had been extubated with ease and lay waiting for us in her corner of the NICU pod with her brand new feeding-tube access button implanted in her stomach lining.

We were pleasantly surprised, but not for long. Avery contracted an infection in her new opening within forty-eight hours and screamed constantly for entire days. She also began to vomit forcefully. We were told that she was merely adjusting to having a feeding tube, but that was only partly true.

I still pleaded with God to heal her, but part of me believed that He wouldn't intervene. When we learned about the hydrocephalus that was slowly increasing in her brain, I prayed and waited for the next report to be good, but it wasn't. The fluid was increasing. The following week, the ultrasound to check the fluid level was repeated—and despite my fervent prayers, it increased again and again and again.

Deep inside my soul, each report of increasing hydrocephalus sent waves of terror. I was more afraid of that one report than her unstable airway, heart defect, or kidney defect. Even more than her aesthetic differences, the ominous knowing that had settled into my soul when

Avery was still a tiny body in my womb latched on to intracranial pressure from hydrocephalus as my true enemy.

Though no one on her medical team found the reports terribly concerning, I dreaded what I felt was coming for Avery.

I wish I could have been wrong.

# Chapter 11

Avery was a month old before she met her older brother and sister. Although Macson and Lolly had come to visit me on several occasions, they had never stepped foot on the NICU floor due to necessary restrictions during flu season. My older children had seen pictures of their little sister, but I deliberately prepared my son for her state as we neared the room where Avery lived.

"She needs a lot of support to live, buddy. She's connected to a lot of different machines right now. You remember, we talked about what happened to her head when she was still in my tummy, but she's going to be OK," I said gently, determined not to overreact to whatever his reaction would be. My six-year-old son was quiet and thoughtful as we neared Avery's bed, and I held my breath, waiting for his first thoughts.

"Oh, she's so *cute*!" he said quietly, yet animatedly, reaching up to touch her tiny hand.

"I think so too, buddy!" I exhaled heavily. "I think so too."

Macs and I spent a few minutes beside her bed. He held her hand, and I explained the myriad medical apparatuses in Avery's corner of the room. I knew we could bond over this information since his mind was as curious as my own. I was conducting informal homeschool in the NICU. I explained the types of machines we would need at home to care for Avery and what each of the numbers meant. I had no idea at the time that over the next few years, his quick mind would grasp Avery's care better than some nurses we met and definitely better than almost all of the non-medical adult population.

When it was Lolly's turn to be introduced, she was less impressed with her new sister and more infatuated with all of the medical paraphernalia within her reach, but not in the same way Macson was. Lolly was interested in tearing each piece of equipment apart or putting it in her mouth. My sixteen-month-old—and the busiest baby I have ever met (this is still true, even as I write this almost five years later)—just wanted her mommy to come home, and if that meant this teeny baby came home too, then so be it.

I did come home off and on for a few weeks after Avery was released, but in the first year of her life, I lived more at the children's hospital than at our house. Often, Avery would begin to fail unexpectedly during the night, so I would kiss my older children goodnight and be gone by the time they woke in the morning without giving them any notice. How could I explain to them that this would be our new normal? How could they possibly understand that my sudden disappearance was not abandonment and that tears streamed down my cheeks as I sped away in the darkness?

I was wracked with guilt in those initial days after Avery was born. Cody would bring Macs and Lolly to visit me on occasion during some of our longer admissions, but most of my interactions with my older children happened over FaceTime. And each time we hung up, I had the sinking feeling that I was letting my older children down. I couldn't be in two places at once, and Avery desperately needed me, but I couldn't help feeling as though Macs and Lolly might permanently feel abandoned by their mother. One day, Lolly had been a fifteen-month-old toddler with a pregnant mother, and the next day, I was gone. Not for a day or a week—I was gone for almost a year with the sister she had never asked for and barely even knew. Our bond was severed. Lolly's babyhood had been tragically cut short by this crisis, and my son was going to face huge life changes as a result of my physical and emotional distance as I cared for my fragile baby in the hospital.

I had been homeschooling Macson before Avery's birth, but the frequency of those lessons slowed after her initial diagnosis while I was still pregnant—and then completely ceased after her birth, leaving him suspended in the middle of first grade. I was failing at homeschooling, I was failing at getting Avery to learn how to nurse, I was failing at getting God to intervene the way I wanted, I was failing at my marriage, and I was most certainly failing at motherhood.

I couldn't believe how rapidly and devastatingly my life had changed. Each member of my family was drowning in some way, and this time, I had done nothing wrong to cause such a crisis. We were a happy family, loving Jesus and loving each other.

*God, You're not only hurting Avery... You're hurting my older kids too. How can You watch all of this and do nothing?*

I was hurt that my God could allow each of my children to suffer so deeply. I was hurt that He had uprooted their lives and separated us. The God I had known was so kind. I was beginning to have trouble reconciling the God I had known with the God who was witnessing all the pain I was seeing and feeling.

The funny thing about God is that He never wastes pain, and the pain He allows is never about one person. He uses pain to shape all of our journeys—and in our case, Avery was the catalyst. Her circumstances were the source of the pain that was interwoven through all our lives. In order for Macson to become who he needed to become, he needed Avery. In order for Lolly to step into her destiny, she needed Avery to be her little sister. My husband needed Avery. As you'll soon see, I desperately needed Avery.

I now believe that pain was the only way. Our pain was not punishment. Our pain was preparation—and for one particular member of our family, this pain was their saving grace.

# Chapter 12

I sat rocking a seven-pound, six-week-old Avery in my arms. We were toward the end of our NICU journey, and Cody and I both felt simultaneously excited and terrified as we prepared to take our fragile baby home for the first time. (Cody would argue that he felt more excited than terrified. I'm not sure he has ever been truly terrified in his life.)

Avery's airway was still an issue because she relied solely on her mouth for oxygen intake, but she had adapted to that advanced style of breathing seemingly well. There had been no dangerous desaturation episodes in weeks, and since we were not ready to choose a tracheostomy for her, our doctors were at a treatment standstill. There was nothing else to do for her but discharge her to largely ill-equipped parents and hope that we wouldn't seriously screw things up.

Because Avery was so medically complicated, she had been followed by nearly every pediatric specialty since birth. Neurosurgery, plastic surgery, neurology, cardiology, nephrology, ophthalmology, pulmonology, audiology, otolaryngology, and gastroenterology, to name a few. With so many hands involved in her care, a fundamental issue arose. Many doctors were concerned with the part of Avery's body in which they specialized, but it didn't seem as though any one particular doctor had a firm grip on how to treat Avery as a whole human being. Also, the specialties did not overlap, so one specialist's concern about a body part not located in their area of expertise could not be addressed for fear of "stepping on toes." Residents didn't disagree with attendings. Specialties remained autonomous, and nurses took great risks whenever they ventured their opinions. It was a system of hospital politics that felt dangerously reckless, and Cody and I were largely uninformed on how to navigate it in a way that served Avery. At the time, I believed that earning a medical degree turned men and women into gods. I believed they didn't make mistakes—and I was very wrong.

When Avery was several days old, an ultrasound was conducted on her head. The images showed that fluid was building up around her brain. Weekly ultrasounds were scheduled to monitor the fluid levels. During our time in the NICU, the quantity of slippery, cerebral spinal fluid inside her ventricles gradually rose, and each week, the ultrasound showed a slight increase in fluid. The last week before Avery's discharge, the fluid level simply "maintained." A doctor told me the increase was barely enough to note. I felt that any increase of fluid threatening to crush my child's brain was worth a note, but what did I know? There was talk of Avery's needing a shunt to drain the excess fluid from around her brain to the free space in her abdominal cavity where it could be absorbed, but the talk never turned into actions.

Something about the fluid and the nonchalant attitude of various specialists bothered me immensely. I couldn't understand how Avery could be discharged if the fluid level had been trending upward for the last six weeks, but we were reassured over and over that discharge was the next right step for Avery. I begged to at least be given a date for a follow-up appointment so that someone with better-trained eyes could check on Avery's progress. We were told to follow-up with our local pediatrician, but the clinic my family attended was a revolving door of random army medical personnel, and my older children were rarely seen by anyone more experienced than a nurse practitioner. We didn't have a regular pediatrician. Avery was being sent home to be fed to the sharks of federal healthcare.

I stated that I couldn't leave the hospital in good conscience without knowing that one of the specialists who oversaw Avery's head, in particular, would be seeing us in the near future. Avery's hydrocephalus had been increasing, after all. Our discharge form gave a follow-up date of six months later. If I was supposed to feel encouraged that Avery's medical team thought I could keep her alive and healthy for the next six months, it did not work.

We sat in the NICU that day, and I pushed my fears aside to take a moment to marvel at how much of a miracle lay in my arms. My new baby had survived a hijacked pregnancy, a dangerous delivery, a host of complications, and desaturations for prolonged periods of time. Somehow she had continued to breathe every day since she had come into the world, and that was an enormous feat in and of itself.

I had already begun writing about her journey and sharing it on my blog in an effort to communicate with our family and friends who had been praying for us and asking about Avery's progress. The blog allowed me to update everyone at once. It was efficient, and I was grateful for the ability to "keep everyone in the loop" with one post, but I did not expect it to spread like wildfire. I was surprised by the messages and emails that began pouring in as our community shared the link to my blog with their friends, and traffic to my website dramatically increased. Hundreds of thousands of people were reading our story. People I didn't know were reporting that they had been deeply touched by Avery's story and inspired to believe for miracles in their own lives. It was just beginning to occur to me that God was using Avery's life for purposes that were much bigger than our little family. Maybe the miracles that He had worked in her life weren't meant for only her. Maybe He was changing the world through the life of a baby who had never uttered a single word or taken a single step.

I began to feel, just for a moment, that maybe all of this suffering had a purpose. Maybe this is what healing really looked like.

Maybe pain wasn't always evil. Maybe good would come from all of this suffering.

Despite my fears, the frustration in my heart eased, and I thanked God for choosing my baby for His cause.

*You are so good to allow these miracles for Your people so that they will remember how powerful You are.*

In that moment and in the face of all my anxiety, I was overwhelmed with a sense of His love for the people He had allowed to read our story.

*Yes, I am good, but these miracles aren't only for other people. I've also allowed them for you so that you won't forget that I'm the One who brought you here.*

The Lord's response sucked the air from my lungs, and I hoped that I was interpreting the meaning incorrectly. We were getting discharged. I was taking Avery home. She would have "a surgery or two" in six months that would fix everything. She was breathing by mouth, so we were not being forced to choose the tracheostomy for her. Avery was getting better. I wouldn't need to remember the miracles because I wasn't going to need any more miracles. Right? A discharge from the NICU meant that Avery was fine. Everything would be easy going forward. By discharging us, the doctors were saying that Avery was safe, that they didn't need to see her anymore, and that they believed we were fully equipped to keep her healthy. Right?

My mind was spinning.

Why would I need to remember? These miracles were meant to change other people's lives. I already believed. I did not need them to be convinced of God's faithfulness. Right?

The knowing descended over my soul like the darkest cloud, and the horizon of my life turned black. My heart told me that this was just the beginning, and tears dripped down my face as I realized this initial hospital stay was just the vehicle to drop my family off right in front of the valley of the shadow of death. I knew in that moment that our journey with Avery wasn't going uphill; we were headed downhill. Thankfully,

I did not realize how steeply we were about to fall—otherwise I might not have had the heart to continue that day.

"Alright," I prayed, feeling the heaviest weight descending on my chest. "Your will, not mine."

God didn't just need me broken. He needed me shattered.

# Chapter 13

The two weeks after Avery's first discharge were nothing like what I had anticipated. I posted a serene picture of her fresh from a bath and swaddled in a blanket with the caption, "We are in the middle of the valley of the shadow of death." Pain had begun to cut away my ability to tolerate or perpetuate anything fluffy or inauthentic. I could only say what was true—good or bad. What was true was that I loved this tiny human more than life itself, but what was also true was the fact that I wasn't sure if I would make it out of this particular valley. This all felt like death and Hell and everything in between.

I thought that once Avery was free from the trappings of the NICU, loosed from the cords and monitors that had entangled her, she would begin to function like a normal baby. She did not. Avery's care was intense and sent our entire family into survival mode even more than being separated from each other during her time in the hospital had. The doctors knew that the care was too much for two parents, so we were told an order for in-home nursing care had been signed, but the paperwork had not been filed. We were sent home believing the request was being processed by our insurance company. We would later find out that no such application had been made, but we carried on believ-ing that we were simply holding on during the interim.

The interim was brutal. Avery's care involved cleaning up a lot of projectile vomit; worrying that she might aspirate, which is espe-cially dangerous for a baby with an inconsistent airway; constantly blaring monitors alerting us to the fact that Avery was in immediate danger; sleeping in "shifts" since she could not be unsupervised for a second, even while sleeping or crying; and listening to her nearly constant screaming.

Most of Avery's first days were spent in panicked screaming fits—hers on the outside and mine on the inside. Her breathing was labored and made worse by her cries, thus increasing her sensation of suffoca-tion. It was a vicious cycle and one that we hadn't seen much in her last few days in the NICU.

Another painful element during that time was that, like any baby, Avery was biologically wired to "suck" as a form of pacification. She constantly cried out, looking for comfort that she couldn't have because her breathing became increasingly unstable with each shriek. The only source of comfort for her was in the tired, helpless arms of her parents. It was torturous. She writhed and clawed at my chest, gnawing on her hands between cries while I sat, desperate yet unable to help her. Avery would go through periods of holding her breath, and I would find myself unwittingly holding my breath alongside her, willing her to take in oxygen. Sometimes she would inhale; other times she would need to be lightly jostled awake and reminded to breathe again.

This went on for almost two weeks. Cody and I slept in three-hour shifts, alternating between Avery's care and that of our two older children. Because I was still pumping breastmilk, my nighttime sleep-ing shifts were shorter—two hours of sleep so I could wake up and pump before taking over from Cody followed by three hours of watch-ing over Avery. When Cody would come to relieve me at the end of my shift, I would have to pump again before collapsing into sleep.

We were beginning to unravel, body and soul, when my parents stepped in to help. My mom and dad began taking shifts together during the night so that Cody and I could sleep for a few extra hours. Ensuring the survival of our baby was a terrifying prospect for two people who had never been trained to care for a child such as Avery, but they knew Cody and I wouldn't last much longer without help. When they began to wear down as well, one of my brothers offered to take a shift. We knew this was not a long-term solution, but we could not refuse the assistance that was helping keep us afloat.

My brother Jon lived out of town at the time, but he would drive for an hour to hold Avery for three hours, then return home to take care of his own family. Two more couples volunteered to help us: the Wigginses—Michael and Anna—and the Rays, Isaiah and Caitlin. Each couple took a shift of holding, comforting, and "lightly jostling" our baby for a few hours so that Cody and I could continue to survive on very little sleep.

I'm not sure how long we could have carried on without this help. These people were the hands and feet of Jesus. They served and loved us by loving our baby into the wee hours of the night and then returning home for less sleep than they were accustomed to before resuming their regular work during the day. Their inconvenience was our saving grace.

Others brought us meals for weeks so that I did not have to cook, which greatly reduced our grocery bill. We were bleeding money in other places, so each contribution of food was a huge help that often brought me to tears.

I do not enjoy asking for or accepting help, especially when I have nothing to give in return, but these people were not asking for anything—they were taking care of Jesus by taking care of His children. Through the faithfulness of a few, God was providing.

I am ashamed to say that I rarely found time to send thank-you notes during those days, partly because I was so dazed by simply staying awake and alive, but also because I did not even know all the different people who reached out to help us during that time. Even in the valley of the shadow of death, He had not left us without help. Jesus, through our friends and family, was caring for us, and in turn, our friends and family were caring for Him. Jesus is always in the valley. I would come to know that the valley is His specialty, the place where He performs His most intricate work.

# Chapter 14

I will forever be haunted by the sound of Avery's ragged, gurgling breaths. In the dim light of the early morning hours, I finally ran out of will to continue our experiment. Avery's ENT had been conflicted about whether or not she needed a tracheostomy but had been willing to let us see how long we could keep her safe without one. Then one day, I gave up.

I wish I had given up that fight much sooner. Cody came to relieve me of my duties that morning, and I told him I felt that Avery had been through enough. So in the darkness of our living room, we made the gut-wrenching decision to get a tracheostomy for our girl. Cody had been convinced that Avery needed a trach as soon as she was born because he felt deeply annoyed by the prospect of having her live in the hospital until she proved she could safely breathe on her own without one, however long that might take. The doctors had mentioned the possibility of Avery's needing a trach to us in a casual way—except for one resident who felt very adamant about the decision. He said the trach was inevitable for Avery and that creating a stable airway for her as soon as possible might allow her to make strides in eating orally, which was impossible as long as she was struggling to breathe. Every other specialist had seemed ambivalent with a "wait and see" kind of outlook on the "trach question."

I had felt that Cody's stance was selfish and that choosing a trach for Avery while she was still breathing well in the NICU was a form of giving up on her. If I could go back, I would elect for Avery to have a tracheostomy on her second day of life. Regardless of whether Cody's perspective was influenced by his frustration, I believe that as Avery's father and the head of his family, he was also divinely inspired. In Matthew 2:13, when God revealed His plan to save newborn Jesus from Herod's jealously, He did not share His plan with Mary. He told Joseph.

The memory of the days leading up to Avery's tracheostomy at eight weeks old—two weeks after being discharged from the NICU—induces a physiological response in me to this day. I find myself holding my breath. I held my breath a lot back then. My baby was so air-hungry and exhausted from her constant struggle to breathe that she screamed almost constantly, since a steady scream ensured a steady flow of oxygen—even if it spent all of her energy to secure it. She would sleep for only minutes at a time before she screamed out again for her next breath, all day and all night.

Thankfully, Avery was so young that she will never remember those days; but for the rest of my life, I will never forget. I'll never forget having to gently shake her from a particularly deep sleep so that she would remember to take her next breath, something her brain may always struggle to master. I will never forget filming the numbers on her pulse ox as they dropped lower and lower so the next attending physician I spoke with would believe me that she was definitely not as stable as they had maintained.

I'll never forget sleeping only three hours a night when Cody would take his shift with her. I'll never forget having to hold her in a very specific position to optimize her very minimal airway behind her obstructive tongue. My arms burned, and my soul ached.

I'll never forget suffering from mastitis over and over because I couldn't pump and hold my gasping infant at the same time, allowing too much time to pass between pumping sessions. I'll never forget feeling too guilty to wake my husband to take over for me because he was also completely exhausted, even as I felt the familiar lumps of clogged milk in my chest. Piercing pain emanated from those red, hardened lumps, and a fever threatened to take hold as I debated how much longer to let my exhausted husband rest in his well-deserved slumber.

I'll never forget making the call that we were ready to choose a trach for Avery and immediately being given a surgery arrival time for the next day. The doctors said they had been awaiting this inevitable decision, and there was no sense in putting the surgery off.

I'll never forget the weight of that choice bearing down on me as I assumed the responsibility of becoming Avery's voice. The procedure I had chosen for her would steal her every sound. To preserve her life, I would make her temporarily mute, not even able to audibly cry.

Avery and I lived in the hospital for several weeks following her tracheostomy. She developed a staph infection almost immediately and remains staph-colonized on her trachea to this day. I began to notice changes in her skull shape, and new bumps appeared daily. I photographed one protruding mound on the left side of her temples and sent the photo to my mom, theorizing that this new accessory was the result of pressure building in Avery's skull. Since birth, both of her eyes had appeared to be bulging, but as her head shape slowly morphed, her left eye began protruding more and more. The entire left side of her face spread horizontally.

She also began to vomit with increased frequency. While she had struggled to tolerate her G-tube feeds since birth, Avery's vomiting became so profuse that the pediatric gastroenterology team was called in for a consultation. They theorized that she had low gut motility, meaning that food passed from her stomach to her large intestine very slowly. This would cause her to lack the adequate space in her stomach for her subsequent feed, resulting in the emesis episodes. Avery was prescribed erythromycin, an antibiotic that would flush the food from her body faster, and Reglan, an anti-emetic drug with a host of sketchy side effects.

I had been prescribed Reglan during my first pregnancy without being educated on the possible side effects. After three days of taking it, I was surprised when the drug induced strange neurological changes: I couldn't access certain words. I first noticed that something was amiss while playing with my nephew, who was a toddler at the time. We were rolling a small red ball back and forth to each other. The ball had rolled a little beyond him, and I tried to tell him to get the ball and roll it back to me, but I suddenly couldn't think of or say the word "ball." I stared at the toy, three feet from me, in total blankness and confusion. A few hours later, I couldn't form certain words with my mouth, as though my brain was losing its muscle memory. Finally, I contemplated harming myself, though not hysterically. The idea seemed very logical to me. I didn't feel sad or sorry for myself, and I was very excited to be a mother, but the thought came into my head, very neatly and without much fanfare, that it might be a nice idea to jump off a very tall building. It seemed sensible, so I entertained the idea warmly for a day before considering that my brain might be sick. I looked at the back of my prescription to discover that Reglan occasionally induced thoughts of suicide and that I should immediately call my doctor if I began experiencing this very serious side effect. I called the office and the midwife repeatedly apologized for not warning me of that possibility, since it had been well-documented and not infrequently reported by users of the drug. I stopped taking Reglan and my brain felt clear within a day.

So now, hearing one of the doctors inform me in her thick European accent that she would be prescribing Reglan to Avery stunned and horrified me.

I said, "No."

The doctor was equally shocked by my immediate refusal and set out to explain what Reglan was and how it worked and how helpful an anti-emetic drug would be for my daughter. I listened, unmoved. When she was finished, I told her that I was familiar with Reglan and its purposes, but she would have to pick another drug for Avery. The entire room was silent for a moment. This doctor was the attending, senior doctor in the room, and in front of a group of residents and fellows—her subordinates—I had gone toe-to-toe with her. She began again, "I don't think you understand…"

I stopped her. "I do understand, and we are not going to use a drug with a black box warning, known for causing serious neurological side effects, *some of them permanent*," I stressed, "on my very likely neurologically compromised baby."

With this statement, the doctor's eyes grew wide, and she stared at me for a moment before relenting. "Alright," she replied, waving her hand in the air as if to say, "Whatever—your loss." But it wasn't my loss, though it very well could have been Avery's.

I decided not to push my luck and didn't contest the idea of long-term antibiotic use, so I made no fuss about the prescription of erythromycin. In hindsight—and particularly when it comes to medically fragile children who become antibiotic resistant very early in life from prolonged exposure to the antibiotic heavy hitters, often developing a severely damaged intestinal microbiome that can contribute to all kinds of gastroenterological upset—I should have contested that choice as well. But hindsight is always 20/20.

Hours later, a beautiful female resident with flowing brown hair quietly tiptoed into Avery's room to see me, closing the door behind her. Despite the fact that we were the only conscious people in the room—and even if Avery had been awake, she still didn't understand English, being a newborn and all—the resident glanced over her shoulder before whispering, "I just wanted to tell you that several of us were so impressed by what you did earlier. We didn't want to use Reglan either. It's not as commonly prescribed in the United States for low gut motility anymore for those exact side effects you mentioned, but she's the attending, so …" She shrugged, and I nodded knowingly. She patted my knee reassuringly before walking out.

I discovered my own voice by becoming the voice for Avery. I only learned how much weight my voice had when it became the primary advocate for my child's life. It had to be honest, hopeful, clear, and unapologetic. It had to be the kind of voice that Avery would be proud to have speaking for her. It couldn't be tainted by my past. It couldn't be whiny or pathetic. It couldn't be weak or inconsistent. It couldn't be cruel or selfish. It couldn't be critical or jealous.

God had given me a story to tell, and now He was beginning to make me tell it, slowly peeling back the hands that I'd purposely clamped over my own mouth for most of my life to keep from rocking the boat. All the pain and suffering was forcing me to speak up and speak the truth, just like it had all those years ago.

✳     ✳     ✳

*Don't puke. Oh my God, I'm going to throw up.*

I plunged into the frigid pool water below, sinking away from the surface, where only moments before, I had been assaulted by someone I knew, who still sat only feet away. I was fifteen years old and on vacation with my family. He was not family, but he might as well have been. I didn't know at the time that what had happened was a sexual assault. I only knew that, in seconds, things had escalated far beyond my control.

*He didn't mean to hurt me. He loves me. It's my fault. I shouldn't have been sitting so close to him. It's fine. He didn't mean to.*

I was fifteen and bleeding, sinking further and further beneath the water. I was too young and confused to make sense of what had just happened. I felt both love and hate, but projected the wrong emotion onto the wrong individual. To him, I had assigned twisted love, and on myself, I had unleashed all of the hate and all of the blame.

*This is your own fault. You were asking for it. If you would only open your damn mouth and tell someone what keeps happening, then this would all stop, but you're too much of a coward. You know once you tell, the whole world will know that you're used goods.*

The familiar claws of shame sank their way into the deepest parts of my soul. This narrative was not new for me. Before I had even had my first kiss, I had been abused on a weekly basis for several years by a family friend and molested once by a stranger. I was used to hiding the truth while drowning in the shame that threatened my very existence.

*If you tell, he'll be in so much trouble. You can't do that to him. He'll lose everything. It's not really costing you that much to stay quiet. If you say anything, then a lot of people will be hurt.*

My face reemerged from the pool to take a gasping breath, but my body stayed underwater. The chilly water helped cool the searing hot pain of newly torn flesh. I was shivering, and yet parts of my anatomy burned as though sliced with a scalpel.

*Maybe if I ignore it, I can make it go away. I know he won't acknowledge that anything happened, so maybe this will all just go away.* These words were well-engraved logic for me. Ignore, suppress, keep quiet, and don't rock the boat.

*I can get over it. It's my own fault, anyway.*

It was the kind of pain that a kid can't make sense of because we were never meant to. So silent pain became both my enemy and my faithful companion, and all I wanted to do was outrun it. I wanted to shut the pain up, and I wanted to starve the hurt out.

*Good luck, Meg. You can run, but you can't hide. The truth will always find you.*

Eventually, the stories we tell ourselves to survive stop working. They run out. The truth has a funny way of crashing into us and forcing us to confront what has been killing us all along. I couldn't advocate for myself yet, but that was a skill I would eventually hone.

For years, I had betrayed myself, but now someone else's life was at stake—and I could not betray Avery.

# Chapter 15

I signed the forms as quickly as I could. I didn't hear a word the home-health nursing supervisor was saying because I didn't care. I believed the nurses who would be coming into our home to assist with Avery after her discharge from the hospital following her tracheostomy would be the answer to all my prayers—the solution to all that ailed me.

I have found that placing that level of expectation on anything in our lives besides Jesus leads to all kinds of disappointment. Home-health nursing was no exception, and as a rule, it initially caused as much trouble as it saved.

The home healthcare agency sent representatives to meet me at the children's hospital to sign contracts and go over the specifics of Avery's care. The doctor who had placed Avery's new airway had mandated home-health nursing to be in place before Avery could be released from the hospital—a step that, she was horrified to learn, was never finalized the first time we were discharged from the NICU. Cody and I also had to be tracheostomy-certified, meaning that we had to show competence in all aspects of tracheostomy care after thorough training.

I felt euphoric. Avery could come home, and we would have a well-qualified nurse to be with her at all times in case anything went wrong. The nurse practitioner in charge of coordinating supplies, training, and home-health nursing at the children's hospital uttered a chilling warning that I didn't understand—until I did. "Not all trach nurses are created equal," she told me in her sharp New York accent. With no frame of reference for such a statement, I didn't even consider that she was trying to prepare me for what might lie ahead.

"What lay ahead" was a special type of horror. At first, I wanted to blame the nursing care agency for the atrocities we experienced, but my perspective shifted gradually over time. The agency could only hire and train certified nurses, but it was up to the nurses to be competent, hard-working caregivers. The agency could not control much of what happened in the home, including when, or if, a nurse showed up for her shift—and in what state of physical disarray or health. (As with Christianity, it's not the system of belief that fails people, but it's usually the misguided, ill-advised attempts of overzealous, overly religious, or ignorant people—but the rest of my thoughts on that are for another chapter.)

The first nurse who entered our home suctioned Avery's trach incorrectly. Because I believed that any mishandling of my baby's tracheostomy might result in her death or, at the least, cause devastating harm, I took this mistake very seriously. I considered that maybe I had misunderstood my own training, so I called the nurse practitioner from the children's hospital who had trained me to double-check. She affirmed my understanding of proper trach suctioning and told me the nurse was operating under the old protocol. And by "old," she meant *very* old. I was rattled by this. How was I supposed to go to bed and sleep easily at night when the nurses caring for Avery might be suctioning my child "the old way"? And why weren't all nurses up-to-date on how to suction a baby?

The next day, the nurse changed Avery's diaper and smeared fecal matter all over her sheets. She did not change the sheets, and she left a suction catheter—intended to be threaded into Avery's trachea—mere inches away. I was bothered to the point of tears to discover this. I had painstakingly organized everything Avery might need in neatly labeled containers so that anyone who walked into my house for the first time would know where to find blankets, sheets, diapers, and any other tracheostomy or enteral feeding supplies, so the fact that she had simply decided not to change the sheets was deeply troubling to me. She only survived a couple of shifts in my house before I called the nursing company and asked that she not be sent to us anymore.

Another nurse lasted a couple of weeks. She was nice and personable, but I began to suspect that she would rather chat with me than actually provide any care for Avery. When Avery developed an infectious rash under her trach ties, I began marking them with a tiny black dot so that I could tell, at the end of the day, if they had been removed and replaced with fresh, clean ones or not. The nurse would report (and chart) that she was changing the ties every day, but, after she left, I removed the ties myself to find the same ones I had marked the day before still around my baby's neck. I called the nursing company again, and she did not return.

One nurse refused to hold Avery. When she screamed, the nurse acted as though she simply didn't hear her. Lolly was a toddler at the time and incredibly busy, so once, when I asked the nurse to pick Avery up out of her bed to comfort her as she cried, since I was engaged elsewhere, the woman told me, "No, I'm too sore from working out yesterday. It was a really rough day at the gym." Since she seemed like a reasonable enough nurse in other respects, I decided that not wanting to touch Avery was not enough of a stain on her nursing skills, so she stayed another week or so—until she decided to touch the wrong child.

Lolly neared the chair where the nurse sat and did something that caused her to lash out (nothing that could harm Avery, since we had kept everything regarding Avery's care far out of reach). The nurse grabbed Lolly by the arm with enough force to leave indented fingernail prints in her skin. Lolly came screaming for me, clutching her forearm to her body. I later learned that the nurse had been investigated for child abuse decades before and that child protective services had removed two of her own girls from her home. She did not return to my house the following day.

One lady sent to our home smelled very strongly of mildew and vomit. She had a kind, grandmotherly way about her, so I instructed my family to ignore the smell as long as she proved to be gentle with Lolly and competent with Avery. Because we had turned our living room into Avery's bedroom, the smell that emanated from the woman made it hard to eat at our kitchen table. When she finished her shift, I found several dead roaches where her bag had been placed. I tried to tell myself it was merely a coincidence, though we had not seen roaches in our house before, but the next day, I watched tiny roaches crawl out from her bag during her entire shift. We called an exterminator to come do an inspection and showed him what the nurse had left behind. "German cockroaches," he told us. "Those things are really bad. If you see one, you're probably infested." We signed up for an extermination plan immediately and asked the nursing agency not to send the woman back. "Let me guess," the coordinator said. "There was a smell. Like mildew and puke, right?" I was horrified all over again.

But one nurse surpassed all others in negligence and danger. She had come into the house complaining of how unfairly she had been treated at her last posting. Before even assessing Avery, she told me all about being asked to leave for sleeping during her shift. "I was closing my eyes for a minute because they were dry and the patient's daughter decided to take a video of me. She said I was sleeping." The nurse snorted in disgust. I didn't really care if she slept as long as she provided Avery with reasonable care. Then the time came for one of Avery's medications to be given.

For my entire life, I've tried to notice things less. I've tried not to notice discrepancies and imperfections and "out-of-placeness." I've tried not to notice when things are missed and balls are dropped, but

I can't. So I learned to pretend I'm not paying attention, but the truth is that I'm always paying attention.

It was ten in the morning, and Avery was due for a particular medication. I knew that the nurse, who had been dozing off and on since she had arrived three hours earlier, had not moved from her chair. As I did every day before each morning shift, I had laid neatly on the kitchen counter the syringes Avery would need for her medication. They had been cleaned and placed at a certain angle so I would know if they had been moved. I paid attention to such details so that I would know the precise moment they had been dirtied so I could wash them immediately, but this compulsivity proved useful in another way.

I waited a little while and then asked the nurse if she had given Avery her medication. I was desperately hoping she would simply tell me no, that she forgot or that she had been too busy sleeping to read the medication sheet and realize that she had missed the designated dosage time. If she said that, I could tell her not to worry about it and give Avery the medication myself. But instead, she blinked up at me and stammered, "Y-y-yes, I did."

My heart sank. "You did?" I asked. "What syringe did you use?"

"That one," she absently motioned toward the tidy row of syringes on the counter. Apparently, the adrenaline surge of being caught in a lie had sufficiently awakened her because she began shuffling through the large black notebook beside Avery's bed with all the necessary paperwork, as though she were suddenly interested in the case. I walked over to the row of supplies to double-check, though I knew what I would find. It was as if my brain had snapped a picture of how I had left things. The photograph was permanently logged in my head and was beckoning me to notice any changes, but there were none. The syringes were exactly as I had left them.

I left the room to ponder my conundrum. Confrontation was one of my worst nightmares. *Don't rock the boat. Don't cause a commotion. Do whatever it takes to avoid making a scene.*

This narrative was old and deeply ingrained, but it no longer served me because it wouldn't work for Avery. I walked back into the kitchen and lowered myself to the level where the nurse sat. "Are you sure you gave Avery her medication? Because you didn't use any of the syringes I laid out. No one has touched them." I looked her directly in the eyes and kept my voice low and firm. She stared at me.

"There's no way you could have given her the medication unless you used one of your own syringes, and you and I both know you couldn't have done that. I need you to tell me the absolute truth so I can give her the dose."

She blinked a few times and then said, "No, I didn't give her anything. The medication sheet said 'miss', so I thought it would be fine if she missed it."

"Miss? Do you mean 'M.S.'?" I asked incredulously.

"Yeah," she said, showing me the medication chart.

"Those are the initials of the last nurse to give her that medication. 'M.S.' They're initials, another nurse's name. They don't stand for 'miss.'"

"Oh," she said.

I tried to let her finish her shift so as to not embarrass her further, but Cody asked her to leave the next time she fell asleep. Apparently, the adrenaline had worn off. She stormed off angrily, cussing at us that she was merely resting her eyes.

"They're very dry!" she yelled behind her as she slammed the door.

Some boats must be rocked. Some whistles must be blown. Advocacy forces us to draw lines in the sand—the lines that force us to confront and let go of our old stories.

Rock the boat. Cause a commotion. Make a scene already.

# Chapter 16

Before Avery was ever on my mind, I felt relatively sure that I had already experienced a lifetime's worth of pain. Two decades before Avery's birth, and despite all my parents' best protective efforts, my five-year-old self slipped through the cracks and into the hands of a predator. My trauma became a homing beacon for broken men, and attracting abusers became my norm. I thought that I was special for a time because grown men, usually strangers, would go out of their way to interact with me.

*Maybe this attention means I'm pretty.* It did not mean that.

*Maybe they go out of their way because they think I'm more interesting than other girls.* They did not think that.

I slowly learned that what attracted these strangers to me was not my effervescent charm, but my damage. And dark, dangerous men could smell my pain from a mile away. As I grew older, sometimes my invisible wounds attracted men who wanted to help me, but I couldn't receive love in a way I did not feel I deserved. The nicer the boy, the faster I ran from him. The better he treated me, the more afraid I was that my past would make him view me with disgust. I felt unworthy of such honest, unselfish love, so I retreated into my cold, distant heart for safety. After all, I didn't know how to love a boy who wasn't intent on using me.

Because I had hidden my experiences, my family operated as though nothing was wrong, oblivious to the fact that before my ninth birthday, I had regularly contemplated the idea of ending my life, anxiously seeking to escape the shameful knowledge that I was different, broken, and used. I was heavily burdened by my secrets, and the guilt of not being perfect weighed on my soul. I was too young, and I had been otherwise too sheltered to even have the terminology to describe what had happened in my life. I sought control and thrived in my quest for perfection. I dabbled in disordered eating and obsessive behaviors, reapplying my nail polish every day to avoid the psychological trauma of a visible chip in the polish.

*If everything looks right on the outside, maybe no one will know what I'm really like on the inside. Maybe they'll never notice that nothing about me is real.*

I was a critical, cynical, jealous, insecure, impossible human. I couldn't compliment other women. I was brutally competitive. I couldn't acknowledge others' accomplishments and success, because if others were doing well, it meant that I wasn't doing well enough. My heart was stone cold. I could never accomplish enough. I could never be good enough. I could never perform my way out of the grotesque darkness of my soul, away from the anxiety of being a worthless failure. I believed that I was ruined, and the only way to outrun the ruin was to hide it and pretend that it had never happened.

My broken grid of lies shaped the way I viewed myself and the world. Even then, my pain was a microphone, and what spewed from my mouth and seeped from my soul was intolerant, judgmental hate—the perfect reflection of my heart. I believed that if I did and said everything right, the pain would eventually heal itself. I believed that if I could fake wholeness long enough, eventually the shattered fabric of my soul would miraculously re-fuse—but as you can imagine, it did not.

The day after my eighteenth birthday, I married my high school boyfriend. I wish I could adequately explain the rationale for that decision, but twelve years later, the full scope of it still escapes me. The relationship had long been over, and yet we remained together as if on autopilot. We had shared an understanding that everyone had been expecting us to marry for so many years that there seemed to be no way out of it. He was much older and had been waiting for me to be old enough to marry since before I was a teenager—a detail I reminded myself of each day I inched closer to adulthood. His waiting seemed so noble and long-suffering—Rachel didn't dare turn Jacob down after seven years (Genesis 29:20). Neither of us was in love with the other anymore, though I do believe perhaps we had been at one time—in a peculiar, chaotic way. We didn't even very much like each other anymore either, but we continued on, as though we were destined to make the mistake. I walked down the aisle with an immense sense of dread, and I walked back up the aisle with a feeling that I had just signed my own death certificate. Marrying felt like a duty that I was bound to perform, and—very unfairly to the man I married—I knew that it was only a matter of time before the end would come, though I was not sure what form "the end" might take. Whether he knew that from the outset as well, I do not know, but he would learn. Rachel would eventually snap, and then she was going to crush Jacob.

Four months after marrying, I conceived my son. I learned this while on a trip during which his father and I discussed getting a divorce. We were staying in a hotel room in Myrtle Beach, South Carolina. He said something about wanting to jump off the balcony (probably because I was always making him so miserable). So I said, with all the coldness I could muster, "That's fine." Our relationship had been so dysfunctional and damaging for so long that my ability to restrain my own venom was waning.

We were in South Carolina for a marathon and could not stand to be in the same room with each other. It did not help that he had been in love with someone else (for some time) who was also on that trip, whom we would see at dinner and during all the other race festivities. He had revealed this fact to me a month before our wedding, but it did nothing to halt what was already in process. I sought counsel, but no one seemed terribly bothered by his admission (or perhaps didn't fully understand the situation and all of its terrible details)—as though it were normal to get married while in love with someone else. I desperately searched for someone to cast doubt on the course we were taking, but no one was troubled by the slow trickle of admissions he made as we neared the wedding. Looking back, I wonder if he was trying to get out as well.

"She's the most beautiful girl in the world," he told me. We had just left a premarital counseling appointment, a box to check for young Christian couples. The humid August air choked me and heat flamed up from my chest as I considered what he was telling me. The fact that he was in love with someone else was not nearly as horrifying to me as the knowledge of who he was in love with. A particular detail about her made my stomach turn, but I wasn't really surprised. I had watched his connection to her grow steadily over that summer. In a way, I didn't blame him. She was indeed beautiful and whimsical and full of young, vibrant life. Her body was long and athletic, not awkward and round like my own.

*This is your own fault. Maybe if you were fun and interesting like she is he wouldn't have had to become so enamored with someone else. Maybe if you ate less and worked out more, then he would love you like he loves her.*

A few nights before we married, we quarreled over the phone. About her. I hung up and wept, but turning back felt impossible. My older sister had overheard some of the fight, and when I hung the phone up, I saw her wince. There was the tiniest bit of doubt in her eyes, but she did not express it. We were all on autopilot.

Right before I walked down the aisle, my father turned to me and said very seriously, "You don't have to do this, you know." But I could not hear him. It was too late to back out now. Jacob was waiting.

The story I held to so tightly—that I needed to go along at whatever cost to keep the peace, to maintain connection, to win approval, to earn love—failed me. It failed everyone back in those days. But in the present, I could not afford to fail Avery. That story had to go.

✳       ✳       ✳

As horribly as some nurses entered our atmosphere, others swept in like a sweet breeze from the ocean on a scorching day. One was a young, single mom. Her previous patient was moving, so she came to us by luck, or really by some act of Divine Providence. She was careful and thoughtful and experienced. She was also very funny, which was very much a plus in my eyes since we spent many hours in the emergency department with Avery together. Knowing that Avery was safe in her care allowed me to sleep deeply and restfully for the first time in months. This woman became our regular weeknight nurse.

Another was a nurse whose previous patient had recently died. She was taken with Avery immediately and insisted on holding her throughout her entire shift, which happened every weekday. Avery grew to love both of the nurses like family, and we held on to both as long as insurance would allow. Gradually, our hours were cut as Avery became more independent, and our original nighttime nurse went to take care of a new family—but perhaps I'm getting ahead of myself here.

In-home nursing was a blessing and also, unexpectedly, a curse. It changed everything about my home. Having strangers in my space at all times left me feeling both overly saturated with interaction and terribly lonely. When I needed to retreat, there was nowhere to go. I had to learn to find peace even when my home was a battleground.

Jesus was waiting to teach me that perfect peace is only found in His arms.

# Chapter 17

It had already been one of the worst weeks of my life. We had only been home for two weeks, and yet again, I was sitting in the emergency room of the children's hospital with my lifeless baby.

Shortly after Avery's tracheostomy, it became acutely apparent that the excess spinal fluid in the ventricles around her brain had begun to crush it as the pressure increased. The bumps I had noted during her recovery from the tracheostomy were portions of her brain being forced out of any available opening in her prematurely fused skull. The excess vomiting was due to increased intracranial pressure.

The fix for such pressure was a shunt—a valve and catheter inserted into her brain to shuttle the excess fluid from her ventricles to the open space in her abdomen, or peritoneal cavity.

Shortly after implanting the shunt, Avery underwent her first reconstructive skull repair, the first of a long series of invasive skull surgeries. The reconstruction was wildly successful—until twelve days into recovery, when Avery's shunt malfunctioned. The hydrocephalus that resulted almost took her life.

With much fighting and advocating and more scene-making than I ever believed I was capable of—because the doctors couldn't believe that Avery was sick instead of merely recovering from a major skull surgery, and because she didn't show the classic signs of shunt infection (we never did find evidence of a shunt infection)—we were able to get Avery into surgery before it was too late. But not before she slipped into a coma in the middle of the night in her hospital room, not before her optic nerves were damaged by the pressure from the fluid-filled ventricles crushing her brain, and not before she suffered brain damage, the extent of which still remains to be seen.

Before the doctors would agree to surgery, they wanted imaging. The scans showed that the fluid in Avery's ventricles was increasing, but the doctors still consulted each other for an entire day about whether to admit her to the hospital or not. Then they tapped the shunt. Once the fluid was removed, Avery slept more comfortably, but she did not regain consciousness. She had not been conscious for almost two days.

Then they wanted to observe her overnight, so she was finally admitted. By the morning, Avery was unresponsive. Cody and I woke to discover this and began demanding to know when someone would intervene. We were told that Avery would have surgery at some point that day, but she could not hold on any longer, and a neurosurgeon finally agreed that the situation had become emergent.

Still, we waited. Avery's room was crowded with young resident doctors wringing their hands when the attending doctor burst in and demanded to know why Avery wasn't already on her way to surgery.

"We're waiting for the transport team," someone in a room full of competent, qualified medical school graduates said.

"This child can't wait any longer!" the attending angrily said. She stormed over to Avery's bed and began tearing the monitor cords from their machines. "I'll take her down myself," she growled as everyone's eyes grew wide.

After the surgery was completed, the shunt was removed, and the fluid had drained, Avery's brain still did not normalize. She suffered from seizures for days. Each episode required emergency interventions as her convulsions made her stop breathing for the duration of the fit. One such episode occurred on an elevator as we descended toward the hospital basement, where the radiology department was housed. Terror and frenzy commenced, and when our elevator ride was over, the nurses and I spilled out of the doors and bent over, each trying to catch our breath.

With each seizure, Avery's eyes would briefly open and stay fixed for a moment before closing. Then she would stop breathing. Chaos to revive her would ensue, and the episode would end with Avery vomiting forcefully. The doctors talked hesitantly of needing to put her on a ventilator.

Our ENT found me in the hallway outside the pediatric ICU relaying this information to my mom over the phone, and she waited quietly until I had ended my update so that she could hear the latest news—even though Avery's brain was not her organ of expertise. When I reached the part about Avery's needing to be put on a ventilator indefinitely, I broke into sobs that wracked my body as the ENT wrapped her arms around me. The prospect of Avery's brain being too damaged to prompt breathing was gut-wrenching for me.

Toward the end of that hospital admission, Avery was still in bad shape and on constant supplemental oxygen, something she had never needed prior to her first shunt malfunction. The ventilator talks never materialized, but I was permanently haunted by them. The images from the radiology department showed a very serious herniation of Avery's brainstem, a condition known as Chiari malformation. Avery's shunt was replaced, but her brain was still very sick. She slept most of the day, and I pumped breastmilk for most of the day. So when I answered a phone call from my husband asking if I was sitting down, I chuckled and answered, "Yes."

*He's trying to be funny, since there's no way anything worse than having a baby in a coma could happen in our lives. Right?*

Wrong.

I had been homeschooling my oldest, Macson, for a couple of years, but after Avery's birth, we decided to enroll him in a private Christian school while our lives were so hectic. He needed to have a physical completed by our doctor, so my husband had shouldered the task of meeting with whoever might be working at the clinic that day. It turned out to be a physician's assistant who made the diagnosis that saved my son's life.

"They found a murmur in his heart, and they think it's serious because his blood pressure was also really high," Cody told me.

I stood to my feet and immediately began pacing back and forth in front of the window of Avery's hospital room. "No, you're joking. He's perfect. There's no way. He's literally perfect. I would have noticed something. Other doctors would have noticed something. How could anyone have missed a problem with his heart like that?!" I struggled to keep the volume of my voice from rising.

"Well, they don't know what it is, but they think maybe it's just a little hole that they can patch up, and then he'll be fine," Cody assured me.

*A little patch job.* The thought comforted me, and we didn't discuss it again until I was able to bring Avery home from the hospital a week later and meet with Macson's new cardiologist.

My son's six-year-old body lay stretched out on the table for the start of his echocardiogram, and I suddenly felt like I was watching the scene before me from a seat on the rafters. *How on earth could my perfect baby be sick?* I had taken him to all of his well-baby visits, and he had been to every check-up thereafter. I had only known Avery to be sick, but the sight of my oldest child's heart in grainy black-and-white images was enough to stop my own. One child with medical issues felt manageable, but two? I was beginning to feel cursed.

The cardiologist didn't say a word but occasionally nodded, as if what he saw had confirmed his suspicions. He turned to me.

"Is there any way your husband can be here?" he asked. "I think you may want him here." At that, I felt sure he was about to tell me Macson's heart was failing, and we were going to need a transplant. (I was about to volunteer my own heart, since I wasn't sure I could survive seeing my baby boy go through something so serious.) But when Cody arrived and we learned that Macson needed one surgery to repair the congenital coarctation—a narrowing of a section of the aorta—I laughed.

"Is that it?" I exhaled triumphantly. The cardiologist looked at me like an alien with no feelings. "No, you don't understand," I chuckled. "My youngest almost died a couple of weeks ago. I can handle a single surgery for Macson. He's not dying, so we're fine."

Further testing would reveal that Macson's heart defects were slightly more complicated than initially anticipated and that his heart was beginning to show signs of stress from living for six years with terrifyingly high blood pressure and an aorta that was both narrowed in some places and dilated in others. We learned that had his condition gone undetected much longer, we were looking at possible damage to other organs and definitely to his heart itself. We learned that in another year or so, he could have indeed needed a heart transplant— and if he had spent another five years without treatment, he could have passed suddenly from heart failure that we never saw coming.

This news changed my heart more than any other news. I knew in my head that God was in control, but seeing how He had so expertly orchestrated our lives to reveal Macson's condition was enough to bring me to my knees in absolute surrender and acknowledgment of His hand in this storm.

Without Avery, I never would have sent Macson for that examination, because I would still have homeschooled him. Without Avery's shunt failing, I would have been home to cancel the appointment my husband insisted on keeping because I had made another appointment for a different day with a different provider. Without all of this, I could have lost my son.

I could see God's hand in this storm. He didn't deal in coincidences, and He wasn't surprised by genetic mutations. He had set my path long before I could see it. He was in control, and I couldn't fight it anymore. Even when my son woke from surgery, disoriented and sobbing that he was dying while my heart broke, I rested in the knowledge that the pain was important and would eventually pass. We would be fine. God was in control.

If only I had always believed that. If only I had seen pain as my friend instead of a rabid dog to outrun. The NICU, the surgeries, the pain and the agony, the anger and the grief—they had all been part of Macson's rescue. Avery and Macson would forever be intertwined. She had suffered, and now he would live. He would suffer too, but none of us would suffer as Avery had.

Perhaps all of Avery's pain had been for good, orchestrated by a good God—not just to save Macson, but also to save her. Maybe all of this pain was for her rescue as well. It was certainly a part of mine.

# Chapter 18

Forty-one days after the initial diagnosis, Macson, Mom, and I checked in for a pre-op appointment at Levine Children's Hospital in Charlotte, North Carolina. Macson's coarctation repair was scheduled for the next morning.

Walking into a facility with which I am wholly unfamiliar is not my favorite feeling in the world, so the stress of handing my son over to his cardiothoracic surgeon was compounded by the feeling of being entirely overwhelmed as I tried to navigate the new terrain. I had spent so much time at the children's hospital closer to our home with Avery that the campus felt like a second home. That provided me with a sense of safety even when she was in critical condition. I didn't have to expend much mental energy worrying about my surroundings. I could be present with her while everything else operated on autopilot. At Levine's, I felt as though I were starting from scratch. Everything about the place felt too big, too scary.

The staff was very helpful and accommodating, but it never felt like our home hospital. We were taken on a tour of the surgical floor, Macson had his blood taken, and I signed all the necessary paperwork before heading to our hotel room for the night. On the outside, I was the perfect cool customer, but my anxiety manifested as horrible, restless sleep. The next morning, someone from the hospital called to say there had been an issue with the first surgical case of the day and wanted to know if Macson was prepared to head in early for his surgery. Luckily, he hadn't had anything to eat or drink since the night before, and I was ready to get the surgery over with, so we agreed and quickly headed to the hospital.

The rest of the morning was a blur. We met with a Child Life specialist, who explained to Macson what he could expect when he woke from surgery and how he might feel, while the surgeon talked with me once more to answer any additional questions. I didn't have any, so Macson was given a dose of Versed for light sedation to ensure that he would feel calm while being taken back to surgery. I kissed my baby goodbye, and he was led away. He turned once to wave goofily at me.

After the surgery started, one of the nurses brought a small plastic box to me that contained Macson's two top teeth. They had to be pulled out as he was being intubated. A wad of cash was taped to the top of the box. The team of anesthesiologists and nurses present during the intubation had all donated the cash they had in their pockets along with a silly note from the Tooth Fairy. While I was sad that his teeth had been lost in that manner, I was both touched and tickled by the gesture. The Tooth Fairy had really set the bar high with that payoff!

The next time I saw Macson, a machine was breathing for him. I walked into his room in the cardiac intensive care unit and felt a wave of nausea rush over me. I had seen Avery on a ventilator before, still and looking lifeless, but seeing my son ghostly white from blood loss and kept alive by technology took my breath away. I had only known Avery as fragile and broken, but this skeletal boy lying under thin white sheets in front of me had been cracking jokes and pestering his sister just days before. This was the boy I had loved more than anyone else in the world. Months before, he had been splashing through the surf in the ocean, and now he did not move when I kissed his cheek.

Because of Macson's size, the surgeon was able to operate on his aorta through an incision between the ribs, known as a thoracotomy. A smaller child would have needed a full, open-heart surgical approach, so I felt grateful at the sight of my son's pristine chest. The resident doctor gave me a rundown of what to expect for recovery.

"I need to tell you that a thoracotomy is one of the most painful procedures a person can have. In terms of pain, it's worse than a sternotomy. Your son is going to be in agony for a few days."

*Great. So much for that pristine chest.*

The doctor also explained that the main concern for the next two days would be managing Macson's blood pressure. His heart had become accustomed to using a certain amount of force to push his blood through the narrowed section of his aorta. Changing the pressure, as we had, might cause the heart to respond by practicing the opposite extreme and not pumping the blood forcefully enough. We also needed to watch the output from his chest tube to make sure the resected portion of the aorta didn't tear and begin hemorrhaging blood. As if that information weren't enough to cause a good deal of concern, Macson would also be at risk for pneumonia from prolonged ventilator use. Because breathing and coughing would be so excruciating after surgery, he might resist doing both of those things, allowing fluid to build up in his lungs.

Simple, right?

Now that you've read a little about my life, you've probably already predicted that at least one of those complications would occur, and if you did, you are not wrong. My mom left the hospital to check out of the hotel where we'd stayed the night before, so I was alone when Macson's alarms started to blare harshly. Usually, when something is going wrong with a patient, the alarms sound softly at first and get louder as things become more critical. In Macson's case, I was startled by how the intense beeping began immediately. I looked at the container beside his bed where his chest tube emptied its contents. There was minimal blood, so I knew he wasn't hemorrhaging and his oxygen levels were fine.

*Umm, yeah, he's on a ventilator, so his body is being oxygenated no matter what.*

That's when I saw it. The room was already full of medical professionals lowering his bed and moving faster than I had ever seen nurses or doctors move when I realized what was happening. Macson's blood pressure, which was continually being monitored by a central line, was steadily dropping. His heart rate slowed. His systolic pressure was at forty. Then thirty. Less and less blood was pumping to his organs and brain.

I remember slowly stepping backwards until my back reached the wall, standing opposite Macson's bed. I knew the team needed to work. I have no memory of what they did or how long this episode lasted; I only recall saying to myself, *Do not cry. Do not make a sound. If you panic, they'll make you leave the room, and then you won't be next to him if he dies.*

This was old trauma programming. *Don't cry. Don't draw attention to yourself. Maybe if you don't acknowledge the fact that your son might be dying before your eyes, you can escape it.* When would I learn that there was no escape?

Whatever was done to save Macson worked. I can only imagine that it was some sort of pressure-raising and blood volume–raising drug cocktail given to him through his IV. Macson was again stable, and I was again alone in his room across from the nurses' bay.

I sank down into a chair and stared at my son for a long time. God had asked me to surrender Avery into His hands, but now He wanted my boy too.

I thought of a quote by C.S. Lewis, one of my favorite authors, from his book *Mere Christianity*. "Nothing you have not given away will ever really be yours." My life was just like that. By holding so tightly to my children, I had turned them into tiny idols, and now God wanted them back, perhaps completely out of my world or perhaps not. Whatever the case, He was tapping me on the shoulder with a question that He had already asked me years before.

*Meg, do you trust Me?*

My children had never been mine to begin with. They were only ever on loan from the One who knew their names before the creation of the world—the One who had knit them together in my womb. I was only ever merely a steward.

*Yes, I trust You. My children are Yours.*

# Chapter 19

My alarm went off at 5:00 a.m. Three hours of sleep had passed in what felt like a split second. I didn't usually sleep for such a long stretch at one time, due to the fact that I was still pumping for Avery (information that, I imagine, is getting very old, but it is important to note for reasons which will be revealed later). I hadn't gotten settled in my room until 2:00 a.m., so I felt fine about sleeping for the extra hour.

The room was pitch black, windowless, and sparsely decorated, but it felt like the most extravagant luxury at the same time. Macson had undergone his coarctation repair the previous day, and I had anticipated an awful night's sleep on a cot in his room in the cardiac ICU. But late in the evening, the hospital staff had informed me that a family room had become available, and I could stay in a small, private room with an attached bathroom for the night. There were a limited number of family rooms, so I knew I was being offered a precious commodity and eagerly accepted. The center of this particular intensive care unit housed a row of small spaces for the families of children who had recently been operated on or were too sick to be moved to regular hospital floors. The private chambers were intended to provide a moment of respite, an escape from the constant droning of medical equipment, and their location provided a sense of safety. The quiet room where I slept was mere feet from where my precious son lay. Macson was sedated and had been on a ventilator since the previous morning, so I knew he wouldn't need me overnight, and the staff assured me they would come get me if he took a turn for the worse.

I quickly showered before falling asleep, thinking of how little things like showering become magnificent blessings when you're living in the intensive care unit. Every shower, every second of sleep, simply lying down when you've been on your feet all day—every luxury felt so lavish.

*If only I had savored simple things in my life this way before everything went south*, I thought. This would be one of the million times during those days when such a thought would make me determined to notice the simple, beautiful things in my life more often. I had taken thousands of showers without considering how grateful I was for them. Perhaps I hadn't ever really been grateful before. Perhaps the abundance had kept me from seeing how incredibly full my life actually was. I fell asleep in seconds.

The plan was to extubate my son that morning at six after a day of medically induced rest. My alarm roused me in time to get ready and do my morning pump for Avery's milk at Macson's bedside before things became hectic. I knew once he was awake I would be busy, so I settled on the seat in the corner of his isolated room to pump and eat a breakfast bar in peace.

Peace. I never would have thought such a thing could exist in a hospital where your child had recently been cut open, where his ribs had been wrenched apart and his aorta had been clamped and cut. I had previously thought that peace was a destination to be reached once everything in life had been sorted out. My vision of peace was a beach in paradise where I could sit, holding hands with my husband while sipping something sweet and cold, and yet here I was finding small moments of supernatural calm in a place littered with the broken bodies of children who might not recover. The morning before, that same room had seemed to be spinning as I watched my son's blood pressure and heart rate drop to terrifying levels. It felt so ironic that this was the same room in which Jesus's Presence now blanketed every crevice. It dawned on me that His Presence had also filled the room the day before, but that my terror had kept me from sensing Him.

Discerning that Divine Presence is like a muscle that becomes stronger with exercise. It seems to me that perhaps finding peace is not a permanent destination, but a transient ebbing and flowing. Experiencing it is dependent on the recipient's resolve to find it. We have to search for it every day as though we've never found it before. Peace is always available if we learn to resolutely look to our Savior even in the scariest of moments and in the most terrifying places—although it takes practice to find Him there.

I had been getting lots of practice.

Because no one was particularly excited to extubate a small boy after a major surgery at the end of their twelve-hour overnight shift, Macson's time was pushed until after seven that morning. This gave me the opportunity to watch the sun rise through the massive bay window spanning his expansive room. That early morning was a rare moment of quiet in my physical space, as well as in my heart and mind. The rising sun splashed beautiful pink and orange hues around the hospital room, and I caught sight of my reflection in the glass window.

I was calm and steady. Even in the hardest year of my life, I was focused and resolute. I wasn't fading in this fire—I was coming alive.

New muscles of faith and confidence rippled in my soul. It was as if parts of me that had been shattered as a child were fusing back together. Advocating and caring for my children had forced me to look away from my failures and inadequacies. I didn't have time to consider how weak or overwhelmed I felt. I didn't have time to consider myself at all. When I finally took stock of who I had become, as I sat in the cardiac ICU that cold November morning, I realized—*I'm stronger and more powerful than I've ever been. I see what You've been up to, God!*

I chuckled. I liked it.

# Chapter 20

After a week at Levine Children's Hospital, Macson and I were anxious to be reunited with the rest of our family. Our local pediatric cardiologist conducted all of our post-operative check-ups to save us any subsequent commutes to Charlotte. We never saw that hospital again. I was so used to complications after each of Avery's surgeries that I kept my suitcase packed for another month, but we never needed it.

Macson's surgery was successful, and his recovery was seamless. He was on strict bedrest for two weeks and required careful bathing to avoid wetting the two fresh wounds on his torso—one a curved, six-inch line following the slant of his ribs on the left side of his back, and the other a two-inch horizontal line where his chest tube had been threaded into his thoracic cavity. Macson was prescribed blood-pressure medicine for six months to guide his body into stabilizing on its own. He required frequent checks of his blood pressure in four key points—both arms and both legs. Once a year, he has the four points checked again, and I hold my breath, willing the right numbers to appear on the screen. High blood pressure in any of his extremities would mean that his aorta has narrowed again, necessitating another surgery.

Macson's heart condition is chronic. In addition to the fact that his aorta could revert to its old, narrowed shape or dissect at the anastomosis (the point where his aorta was cut and sewn back together), his aortic valve is leaky and functionally bicuspid (as opposed to tricuspid). His valve could require surgery, or merely medication, or be asymptomatic for the duration of his life, so there is no way to anticipate the interventions his heart may need in the future. He will have to see an interventional pediatric cardiologist (yes, pediatric, since his condition is associated with childhood) every year for the rest of his life to monitor his baseline. And because he lived for six years with an untreated coarctation of the main artery in his body, his aortic root must be routinely measured.

During Macson's first CT scan after the diagnosis, it was discovered that the section of aorta directly in front of the coarctation had begun to dilate as the pressure built in his veins. His heart grew a web of collateral veins around the area to shunt the pooling blood elsewhere, but the dilation still occurred and could pose a great threat in the future. The final concern is that children who are born with coarctation of the aorta are at increased risk of developing brain aneurysms.

Recently, Macson went through a period of experiencing blurry vision and vomiting from migraines. Waiting for the scan of his brain was tortuous, but it revealed that he has yet to show evidence of aneurysms. He'll need regular imaging to check for developing aneurysms once he reaches his teenage years, but until then, I just get to feel a tiny bit of terror each time he complains of a headache.

It's a constant exercise to hold my children's futures loosely in my hands. It's a constant reminder that I am never "in control."

✳    ✳    ✳

Avery was still recovering from her shunt malfunction that had occurred that August, and Macson was bedridden from heart surgery that had just occurred in November, so they convalesced together. Avery was taking Kepra for seizures, Macson was ingesting Amlodipine for blood-pressure management, and I was administering both medications myself to avoid any errors.

The year 2015 drew to a close and brought some exciting changes. Avery no longer showed any signs of seizures, and we were able to wean her off her medication. Macson was given a clean bill of health and returned to school.

Because both children appeared to be stable, Cody and I decided to take the entire family on our first trip. I was intimidated by the thought of venturing outside of our usual area, but the rest of my family was spending Christmas in Williamsburg, Virginia, which is particularly magical at Christmastime, so we decided to take the risk. It paid off. As if to signal that we were making the right decision, Avery decided to surprise us by holding her head up for the first time on Christmas Eve. She was nine months old.

Lolly and Macson were visibly relieved to be participating in some holiday normalcy, and the trip went surprisingly well.

The joy was short-lived, however. Shortly after New Year's Day in 2016, the bottom dropped out, and all my hopes of moving on from the darkness of 2015 were dashed.

# Chapter 21

The room was dark and silent, other than the sound of Avery's raspy, gurgling inhalation and exhalation. I lay inside the walls of the hospital yet again, though in a very different unit than the one I had stayed in during Avery's recovery from her tracheostomy. Before the lights had gone out, I noticed that the accommodations were not much different than a hotel room. A single bed, sparsely clad with a lone sheet, two thin pillows, and a scratchy blanket, was flanked by a hospital recliner on one side and a side table on the other. A large painting hovering above the headboard concealed an interior crevice that housed resuscitation equipment in the event that any of this room's visitors ceased to breathe during their sleep.

Avery lay in a hospital crib nearby, covered in wires. Censors tracked her brain waves and eye movement. Stickers attached to plastic tubes measured her heart rate, breathing patterns, and exchange of oxygen, and a small camera on the ceiling tracked her movements, watching for frequent leg twitches or any other unusual physical behaviors during sleep.

This was her third sleep study, and it was as uncomfortable as the last. The previous results had given us some grave news about her brain and answered the troubling mystery behind her increasing need for supplemental oxygen while she slept. But I lay hopeful on this night because I thought we had solved the problem with her latest surgery.

Right? Wrong.

Weeks before this study, Avery had been medically induced into sleep and sliced with a scalpel yet again. An MRI taken during her last admission after her shunt tragically failed had shown us that she suffered from a rare brain condition known as Chiari malformation, a structural defect of the cerebellum. Her case was particularly severe because along with the herniation of her brainstem through her foramen magnum, a portion of her cerebellum and fourth ventricle was being forced down through the base of her skull. The portion of her brain that controlled basic functions such as breathing, swallowing, heart rate, blood pressure, central nervous system expression, consciousness, and sleep was being wrenched and crushed by her skull and cervical spine. The pressure was putting strain on Avery's brainstem, inducing significant pauses in her breathing—pauses long enough to drop her oxygen into dangerously low territory, causing the new need for oxygen at night. We had been advised to begin using a ventilator for her while she slept to support her airway more effectively, as all the oxygen supplementation was causing hypercapnia—slow carbon dioxide poisoning. Oxygen was being pumped into her as she slept, but her brain was forgetting to initiate enough exhales, allowing carbon dioxide levels to rise in her body during the night.

The ventilator put us one step closer to artificially prolonging my precious baby's life. The ventilator was a machine I might one day have to choose to turn off. It was a constant, visual reminder that my profoundly broken child might one day slip from my hands. The ventilator was my enemy.

Surgery was imperative because Avery's basic functions increasingly suffered, and possible paralysis loomed overhead. Compression of the nerves and membranes of her spinal cord made total physical disability likely and rapidly approaching.

In February 2016, the neurosurgeon had sliced open the back of Avery's skull in a six-inch vertical line to expose the base of her brain and cervical spine. He had removed small chunks of bone from the arched top of her spinal canal and shaved away portions of her cervical vertebrae to decompress her posterior fossa and allow her brainstem space "to breathe." If circumstances were favorable, he also planned to cut open her dura, the membranous tissue surrounding the brain and spinal cord, and sew a patch into the dura to expand it—like adding a piece of elastic to the waistband of a pair of pants that are too tight. Because babies have notoriously vascular dura, we knew that procedure could carry great bleeding risks, and Avery was no exception. When the surgeon removed the bone from the base of her skull, he found that Avery's dura resembled a blue lake; cutting into it could result in her rapidly bleeding to death. No duraplasty was performed, which meant the decompression surgery would be less effective and would likely need to be repeated at some point in the future.

Special care had been taken to monitor Avery's nerves during the procedure. Her head and neck had been situated in a certain way to allow the surgeon to operate, but the prolonged compression of the base of her skull during the surgery could have rendered her paralyzed regardless of the decompression—or worse, simply unable to ever wake again. Her nerves were watched closely so that the surgeon would know to abort the surgery if the damage was becoming too severe.

The surgery had been successful, so we were repeating the sleep study, hoping and praying that the decompression of her brain stem would lessen the need for oxygen and solve the problem that plagued her. Immediately following her brainstem decompression, we saw what we felt was great improvement in Avery's apnea, so we were very hopeful for good news.

Days later, however, I received a call that would plunge my soul into great darkness. The results of the sleep study showed that Avery's number of central sleep apnea episodes (known as an AHI) had increased since her previous study. Despite her recent surgery, her number had gone from thirteen to twenty-two episodes an hour.

I felt my heart drop into my stomach as I begged to know how we were going backwards. A brain that was worsening despite our surgical interventions sounded like a brain in a state of degeneration.

My mind spun wildly out of control, and no medical professional could help me make sense of the news. Honestly, and to their credit, the professionals didn't even try. No one had concrete answers. Those were impossible at this stage, especially regarding the human brain. Avery was diagnosed with severe central sleep apnea, a condition with no treatment besides the use of a ventilator connected to her tracheostomy for the rest of her life.

"You mean, she may need the trach forever?" I asked with a hint of a snap. We had only been prepared for Avery to need it for several years.

"Yes, if she does not outgrow or recover from her apnea, she will be on the ventilator, with a trach, for the rest of her life," I was told. This answer left me indignant.

"You're telling me there's really nothing we can do?" I asked angrily. "No medicine, no therapy, no surgery—nothing? You're telling me that in a world where someone figured out how to help Bruce Jenner surgically become Caitlyn Jenner, you can't do anything to fix this so she won't be on life support for the rest of her life?"

"Yes. There's nothing to do but wait and see."

I was furious. I was defeated. I could not make sense of how a country that boasted such amazing medical advances had no answers for a diagnosis that seemed so simple and straightforward. We were making no progress. The surgery hadn't helped and, in fact, Avery's brain was regressing. For all her external improvements, her brain was in great turmoil either because her Chiari malformation was too symptomatic or, more likely, because the chronic pressure on her brain from hydrocephalus and the acute episodes of shunt failure that had marked her first six months of life had damaged it beyond repair.

Damage that could only be realized by the "wait and see."

I pictured Avery as an adult, needing to be suctioned throughout the night. I pictured myself twenty years down the road, bleary-eyed and depressed, listening to the alarms of the ventilator signaling another apneaic episode.

*Oh, God—have mercy.*

The unknown was terrifying. The wait-and-see was excruciating. The helplessness was debilitating.

Once and for all, God had removed my control over Avery's future. He had removed my control over my own future, and He wanted me to be OK with it. He was waiting for me to break. He was waiting for me, without hesitation, to say, "Our futures are Yours, with or without a trach, ventilator or no ventilator. You are good, and You only do what is right."

Those sentences are more easily typed than believed.

My dreams, my timeline—all of my visions for the future were dashed. It wasn't supposed to go like this. It wasn't supposed to be this hard. It was supposed to just be "one or two surgeries."

It was supposed to be simple craniosynostosis.

# Chapter 22

The news of Avery's possibly permanent need for a trach and ventilator came at a particularly traumatizing period in her babyhood. As I mentioned before, her Chiari decompression surgery had seemingly been a massive success, but the events that followed momentarily crippled my soul. I slouched onward, but I felt very broken and bewildered by what I had witnessed.

Weeks before, I had donned a mask and gown to be allowed to sit at Avery's bedside. The infectious-disease team had put a sign in front of her ICU room marking it as dangerous, a medical scarlet letter. The sign demanded extreme caution when entering and exiting the sliding door made of thick glass behind which my baby lay.

She had been discharged from the hospital forty-eight hours after her decompression and had recovered well at home for a day or two. She was very sleepy and irritable, but I attributed all of this to an understandably painful recovery. I began to notice small, slightly orange stains on her crib sheets where her head lay, the product of a slow ooze from the incision down the back of her neck. I phoned the neurosurgeon on call at the children's hospital that weekend to tell

him about the discharge, as well as what appeared to be a tiny gap
in her sutures. At the base of the incision, a small hole was appearing,
but the area did not seem particularly red or warm to the touch, so
the doctor told me to keep an eye on it and let him know about any
changes or increased discharge.

A few hours later, there were significant, messy changes. Avery lay
in my arms while I gently rocked her back and forth in the overstuffed,
gray recliner that sat next to her crib. She was calm, though listless.
Her head was positioned gingerly on my right arm, and I cradled her
skull with much caution. Suddenly, as we slowly glided, I felt a gush,
and a fluid and sticky warmth encased my forearm underneath her
neck. I shifted her position in my lap to see what was pouring from her
incision, terrified to find blood, only to discover a pool of orange-tinted,
slippery fluid covering my arm and a portion of the chair. The back of
Avery's outfit was also drenched. I called the neurosurgeon again, and
he advised us to take her to the emergency department at the children's
hospital for an examination. He added that he was aware of Avery's
case and had assisted during her surgery a couple of days before.

When we arrived at the hospital, the surgeon met us, and upon
seeing Avery's fresh wound again, mentioned that he and several other
neurosurgery residents had been encouraged to each place a few stitches
in her scalp. It made sense to me that a teaching hospital would allow
this, but I still found the idea very exasperating.

*How about you practice your stitching on a different body part?
Not the skin directly above my kid's brainstem. Thanks.*

I thought these words but did not say them because I thought they
might make me look bad, though I couldn't help myself from giving
a little jab. "Well, I hope this stitch wasn't yours," I said glumly, pointing to the gaping hole in the series of sutures. Avery needed two
additional stitches to close the hole from whence the fluid was leaking.
I asked if there was any way it could be cerebral spinal fluid. Avery's
dura had been nicked and quickly sewn shut during the surgery, so I
knew that there had been a weakened area, and I wasn't feeling

particularly confident in the whole stitching process anyway. He said it wasn't—that the fluid was most likely blood plasma from a seroma that had formed underneath the incision. The resident proceeded to drain several ounces of translucent orange fluid from the opening in Avery's newly acquired scar.

What happened next was understandable, but it still troubled me deeply. The surgeon needed to add a few stitches to close the hole, so he acquired a syringe of lidocaine to numb the area and sewing supplies. Efficiency is paramount in the emergency department, and time is of the essence, so quick patient turnover can result in some hurried movements. The neurosurgeon was also the only pediatric neurosurgery resident on call and was needed for a consultation on another floor, so I do not blame him for what I'm about to tell you.

Avery had been asleep for the entire visit despite the doctor's poking and prodding on the tender flesh down the back of her neck, but she was awakened with the sharp jab of a needle full of lidocaine into her recently severed skin. The surgeon emptied the contents of the syringe into her incision as she woke with a scream, and then, without wasting a second, he immediately plunged the stitching needle underneath her skin. None of the lidocaine had taken effect, so my fragile baby continued screaming. She thrashed and contorted her body with a physical desperation that I had never seen in her before. Cody held her down so that the doctor could finish sewing, and I helplessly held on to her foot, repeating, "Just pass out, just pass out, baby," while praying that her body would protect itself by simply losing consciousness.

Avery finally did pass out just as the doctor finished his task. He hurried away as I gathered my deeply worn baby into my arms, bundled her in a blanket, and took her home. As we sped away on that frigid, dark night, I remember hoping that this would be the end of our time in the hospital for a while—but God was about to allow one more malady. And this next foe would be the one that would finally force me to commit my baby to His arms. I would finally pray, releasing her to Him to take home for healing.

"Don't leave her here for my sake. If it's home that You want her, then take her. She was never mine anyway. She shouldn't have to suffer like this anymore. However You heal her, please just heal her, even if the next time she wakes up, she's waking to meet You."

# Chapter 23

And now we have come full circle from where we began this story. As you might remember, our night nurse, Bea, woke me up the following night because something was not right with Avery.

She hadn't been herself since the surgery, but even in the dim light of the family room that had become her bedroom, I could see that my baby was miserable. Avery lay screaming in her crib. I checked all the various spots on her body that might indicate what was wrong but could find no clear culprit. I decided to take her to our local emergency department, the small army hospital situated in the middle of the large military installation near our home. The staff did everything they could to meet my needs, but after only a few hours, they had exhausted all the possible treatment avenues—leaving me with no choice but to take Avery back home for further observation. If she stayed uncomfortable, I would have to take her to the children's hospital again. The thought of driving to that emergency department for the second time in three days, only five days post-op, seemed a little silly and excessive.

*Don't be an alarmist, Meg. You'll get a reputation at that hospital if you're not careful. They'll think you panic about everything, and they won't take you seriously.*

Even as I thought these words to myself, my mind drifted back to other times when I had taken a doctor's reassurance or nonchalance as law and not pushed harder when I felt that my baby needed to be treated more aggressively. Avery's eyesight had been permanently damaged due to some of my previous compliance. My stance with the doctors had become more and more aggressive, regardless of whether that made me seem difficult or notorious. I couldn't go along to get along. I couldn't keep everyone happy. I couldn't avoid making a scene, and I couldn't lie when I felt so strongly—when the knowing of danger made me feel almost sick—any longer. I could not back down. I could not discount myself ever again.

By the next afternoon, Avery was increasingly difficult to rouse from her near-constant sleep, and when she did briefly open her eyes, I could tell that she was not "there." "Unoccupied eyes" was the look that I came to know and dread in those first two years after her birth. It was a look that I could not always explain to the doctors, but one I took more seriously than any other symptom. Following that look has never failed me. Avery's eyes would meet mine, and I could tell that she couldn't see me. Those big brown eyes, surrounded by the longest, thickest, most beautiful eyelashes in the world, were blank, dead, lifeless, like eyes that you would see on a mannequin or a baby doll. Colored circles with nothing animated underneath. She showed no recognition, nor did her eyes communicate any pain or desperation.

I learned during those years that an angry baby is a viable baby. A child that is screaming in pain still has some fight left in it. The child may be uncomfortable, but it is still strong enough to contest. A baby that stops screaming in agony to retreat into limpness is a baby that is succumbing to its foe, a baby that is slipping behind the veil.

Avery's eyes met mine, and even her pain made no effort to talk. That's when I knew. The life was sliding out of her, and if I didn't get help immediately, it might be gone for good.

As soon as my parents arrived to stay with our older children, Cody and I loaded Avery into the van and sped toward the children's hospital. Her condition did not clinically warrant an ambulance or a helicopter ride, but time was still of the essence. The conundrum was this: Although she was slipping from consciousness, her heart beat steadily. It beat faster than normal, but it continued to beat at regular intervals. Her oxygen levels also remained level. I knew that on the surface, she looked to be sleeping peacefully, so I needed to prepare my case to present in the emergency department. I arranged the details of the last five days neatly and efficiently in my mind, and then I raced Avery inside as soon as we arrived while Cody found a parking spot. As usual, Avery's appearance secured us a curtain in triage very quickly, but then we would have to wait our turn to speak to a doctor like everyone else. By the time the resident came in to examine Avery, I had my spiel down.

I told him how she had been operated on five days before. Three days later, we had returned to the same department in which I now sat for additional stitches due to an aggressively draining seroma. The following night, I had taken Avery to our local hospital for IV fluids, a chest X-ray (which showed no sign of post-surgical pneumonia), and blood work, which showed a slightly elevated white blood cell count of nineteen. I ended my speech with what had brought us in that day.

"I know she probably doesn't look like a baby who is deathly ill, but I know her better than anyone in the world. Something is not right, and I won't leave here until we've solved it."

As soon as I had finished speaking, almost on cue, Avery's pulse-ox began to beep, slowly at first and then faster. Her heart rate was climbing higher, and her oxygen was dropping.

The young doctor who had been listening to Avery's lungs immediately stopped. He slung the stethoscope around his neck and lifted her pinky finger. He squeezed it and quickly disappeared behind the curtain. He appeared moments again with the attending doctor overseeing the emergency department that day. She was a middle-aged woman with dark brown hair clasped in a low ponytail. She did an abbreviated exam of Avery and then began giving orders to admit her and start antibiotics immediately.

"Get this baby to the ICU," she said as she turned to leave. The doctor stopped and looked over her shoulder at the machine attached to the wall that showed Avery's vital signs. "And it looks like she's going to need to get a ventilator," she added.

Avery's body had turned gray and was shutting down. At nearly a year old, it was slowly losing its ability to oxygenate efficiently. The broad-spectrum antibiotics could fight a number of infections—and the sooner they began pouring into her veins, the better.

Measuring the lactic acid level would determine the rate at which Avery's organs were failing—a gauge of how far gone she was. The ventilator was meant to ease the strain on her body of having to breathe. The machine would breathe for her so that her body could try to fight the infection if it could summon the strength.

Avery was entering a battle into which I could not follow. I had done everything I could do except completely let her go. So I committed her back to her Creator and released my white-knuckled grip.

Being her advocate was my only job. It was the only thing I could control. I had to be as strong and as firm and as determined as I could be. I had to make my case and force the hands of the professionals if necessary, but I couldn't heal her. I had to be satisfied with how fiercely I had fought for her, and then I had to sit and wait. Avery and Jesus would decide her fate now.

*Do you trust Me?*

# Chapter 24

Waiting for Avery to live or die gave me time to consider the short life she had led that I was so honored to have witnessed. She had already endeared herself to so many with her squinty smile and enormous cheeks. She had not yet learned to speak, but she let out tiny squeaks of air around her trach tube to communicate excitement or frustration. Though her fists remained clenched (a sign of neurological damage), she could wave and shake her head "no." A social worker had gifted Avery a plastic frog after her last surgery, and while she could not manipulate the frog herself, she burst into an enormous grin whenever she saw it.

On good days, she was able to roll from side to side. On bad days, like the ones in which we found ourselves in February 2016, we waited for the medical professionals to give us a clue as to whether we might be leaving the hospital soon—with or without Avery.

"She isn't getting worse, which is a great sign," the attending doctor told us each morning during rounds. "She's holding steady. Let's see how the day goes."

Rounds (discussions or updates about each patient under the attending doctor's care) occurred early in the morning right outside the sliding glass door of Avery's narrow room in the intensive care unit. A handful of doctors, mostly residents, would present Avery's medical history and current state to the senior doctor who oversaw each patient on the entire floor. A nurse and various other specialists involved in Avery's care, sometimes a nutritionist or physical therapist, would stand in a cluster to discuss how she had fared overnight and what the treatment plan would be for the day. Avery had been admitted to the hospital with sepsis—an infection in her bloodstream—a few days after her Chiari decompression surgery and had been in critical condition since then.

"Avery Apperson. Eleven months old. Admitted to the hospital five days ago with possible infection of the bloodstream. Eight days post-op for a sub-occipital craniectomy and cervical laminectomy," someone would begin. I would wedge myself into the cluster and wait to offer my two cents. I knew I carried vital information, and I felt competent enough to share it. I knew that Vancomycin gave Avery red man syndrome (an anaphylactoid reaction), that she couldn't tolerate certain pain medications, and that she would respond better to Tylenol than Oxycodone. I knew the rate at which we could reintroduce feeds with calculated precision—and I was the absolute earthly authority on reading her cues in healing or decompensation.

Days earlier, during the initial frantic afternoon in the emergency department, I had texted my mom that things were not looking good for Avery. She and my dad surprised us later that night by appearing in the waiting room where we sat, unable to see Avery until three doctors had finished drawing cerebral fluid from her spinal column. A spinal tap was considered a surgical procedure, so the room was sterilized and the practitioners wore masks and gowns. Cody and I were not allowed to observe.

My parents had secured childcare for our two older children and driven an hour and a half in the middle of night to hug us and possibly see Avery for the last time. Only two visitors were allowed in her room at a time, so once we were informed that her procedure was finished, Cody and my dad went in to visit with Avery while my mom sat in the waiting room with me until it was our turn to sit by her bed.

That night, my dad promised Avery that when she survived the infection and after she had learned to walk, he would take her to Walt Disney World. "We'll call it Avery's Trip," he told her, although she was not conscious to hear him. He came back to the waiting room and shared his plan, and I teared up thinking about how I had stopped considering what life might be like on the other side of this crisis.

Who would Avery become if she lived through the night? What Disney princess might be her favorite? Would she ever learn to walk, or would I push her wheelchair through the theme park? I wasn't sure if or how I would answer any of those questions that cold, February night, but I did know one thing:

I wanted Avery to go to Disney World.

# Chapter 25

After a week of uncertainty in the hospital, Avery survived sepsis. The origin of the infection that overran her bloodstream remains a mystery to this day, but some fearsome malady triggered a severe inflammatory response in my baby that nearly stole her life. For days, we waited for signs of improvements, and for days, she gave none. She slept day and night, and the color of her skin remained sallow. Because the source of the infection could not be found despite several lumbar punctures, X-rays, and urine and stool sample tests, Avery was quarantined out of caution. Cody and I wore masks and gowns and blue latex gloves to sit at her bedside, willing her to improve and open her eyes.

She lay motionless on her left side, puffy from her veins being pumped full of antibiotics and fluids, some of which were seeping into her surrounding tissues. My baby was not even a year old and had suffered through so many surgeries and setbacks that she had not yet had time to learn to sit up on her own. The closest she had come to that milestone was sitting propped up and hemmed in by cushions while still slouched to one side of her highchair. She had barely learned to hold her head up. With each complication, we were moving backward with her physical progress. During each sickness and after each surgery, her body would fight so hard to recover, to simply stay alive, that it couldn't simultaneously develop or even grow. Her stature had been impacted by the seemingly never-ending set of obstacles.

Her feeding progress was the same. We would see small improvements with her constant vomiting, only to find ourselves back in the hospital with Avery on IV nutrition because she couldn't tolerate G-tube feeds due to nausea and vomiting, the side effect of anesthesia or morphine.

Every hospitalization left me feeling like we were back at square one. The only constant element during her recoveries was breastmilk, which I pumped relentlessly to give her through her feeding tube. I believed my milk could support her better than formula could and that somehow, as long as I was providing for her that way, I was contributing. It was the one activity that counteracted the helplessness I felt as Avery lurched on toward health, often at a painfully slow speed. I felt a compulsion to help her in that way, far beyond what was reasonable. For fifteen months, I pumped breastmilk for her, waking in the night to pump even when my body and soul had been stretched far too thin. Ultimately, my compulsive need to do something during that stressful time, with no regard for balance or self-preservation, cost my body and soul very dearly. I reasoned that I suffered out of love, but that is only partly true. I pushed myself so hard out of selfishness too. Pumping made me feel useful, important. It made me feel self-righteous as well. I felt that doing things the hard way made me a better mother, but now I see that sometimes it just made me a tired mother. At the end of my pumping journey, I entered complete physical burnout, a state from which I am still trying to recover four years later.

Suffering for those we love is noble, but so is resting. I might have been able to care for Avery more effectively if I also had been caring for myself.

After days of little hope, as I watched Avery's body fight sepsis with everything it had, her color began to improve. And while she still mostly slept, she did so peacefully. Sleeping while sallow and gray looks like the sleep of someone who is in a coma—not recovering, but hovering. Hovering between Earth and the heavens. That sleep doesn't look like rest; it looks like terrifying stillness. But the sleep into which Avery fell now was restorative. I could tell by the way her eyebrows relaxed. I could tell by the way her hands lay open, not curled and tight. In fleeting moments, it felt safe to believe she might survive, but it still seemed dangerous to think of life on the other side of this crisis.

Once it was confirmed that the source of Avery's infection was not the type to easily infect others, such as an imbalance of the bacteria in her intestines known as C. diff (which is particularly devastating and potentially fatal for small children and the elderly population), the gloves, masks, and gowns were allowed to come off. I could resume pumping by her bedside and holding my sweetly sleeping baby. The doctors still made their morning rounds, baffled by the elusive source of the explosive infection that caused such a strong reaction in Avery's body, but hopeful that she was on the upside of her battle and would eventually be released. The cause of the infection was not as important as whether Avery would be able to beat it—and day after day, it appeared that she would.

One afternoon, we stepped out to eat for a few minutes and missed some visitors, a couple from our church who had stopped by. The ICU nurse caring for Avery that day told me that we had returned just minutes after their departure and that they had slipped away to avoid disturbing us if we were busy. I remember hearing what the nurse was saying until I caught sight of a colorful box on the window of the pediatric intensive care room. The air caught in my throat as I moved closer to it, and I had to stifle tears that threatened to spill from my eyes.

The couple had brought a toy for Avery. Attached to the gift was a small note saying that they were sorry that they had missed us, that they had prayed over Avery for a few minutes, and that they would continue to pray for her healing. Once the nurse had left the room, I started to cry.

I was deeply touched by the couple's kindness and the fact that they had driven a long way to communicate to us that we were not alone. I was even more deeply moved by the gift. Giving Avery a toy meant to me that the givers had faith that my child would live, that she would fully recover and enjoy the toy as an average child would. The faith they had in my baby gave me a renewed perspective.

One day, Lord willing, we would leave that hospital and take our baby home to rejoin her siblings. One day, Avery would be healed. One day, Avery would be well long enough to learn to crawl or sit up on her own. And one day, Avery would go to Disney World.

Avery's eyes fluttered open, and she reached her chubby hand, still in a fist, up toward my face. Her gaze met mine, and I could see that she was lucid for the first time in a long time.

"Hey, sweet girl," I said, taking her dimpled fist in mine and bringing it to my lips. "Guess what? Poppa said he's going to take us to Walt Disney World when you're ready. So, you just focus on getting better, and then we're going to Disney!"

# Chapter 26

Avery was finally released from the hospital one month before her first birthday.

The weeks that followed her return home began a spell of positive progress. The earth was thawing out from a bitter winter, spring was creeping in, and Avery began to bloom right alongside the dogwood tree in our backyard. We celebrated her birthday with a small party, inviting our family and each of the people who had been instrumental in supporting us during the first few weeks of her life, including the people who had come to hold her during the night so that Cody and I could get a little sleep.

Avery was alert and engaged as I helped her open presents and tried to convince her to dig into her birthday cake. She was not able to try even a lick of icing due to her severe food aversion, nor would she tolerate touching the sugary concoction with her hands due to sensory aversions that she had also developed—but she was home and safe. The light had returned to her eyes, and we were blessed with a streak of good health.

Avery began to make real progress. Her core strength and head control improved, and each day we practiced her unassisted sitting. By the end of March, she could sit almost entirely on her own. Her hands began to unclench, and she was able to grasp toys—her favorite of which was a miniature baby doll in a pink, striped suit. The world of play opened up before her for the first time. Different textures and fabrics, squeaky toys and silent toys, all part of a glorious sensory experience that was new and so exciting to her.

We began making a concerted effort to teach Avery sign language so that we could communicate, but she preferred to make noises that mimicked the words I tried to teach her. The doctors had advised us to teach her sign language as early as possible because having a trach should have rendered Avery absolutely mute. But she had other ideas. Gradually, over the next year, the squeaks and sounds she was able to make, despite her trach, morphed more closely into words. I had accepted that Avery would not be able to talk until the day we permanently removed her trach—and possibly not at all, since we were told she might never be able to survive without it—but once again, she was full of surprises.

And this time, in a good way. My baby learned to speak. Single words at first, then phrases, then full sentences. Her speech was hard to discern at first, but it slowly became understandable even to strangers. She was determined to speak. As it turned out, she was determined to do a lot of things she wasn't expected to do.

That spring, we visited a park for the first time, and although Avery spent the entire time safely tucked against my body in a baby carrier, she cautiously surveyed her surroundings and studied the crowd of strangers, occasionally peeking up at me to smile. She loved being outside.

The season around Avery's birthday was full of firsts. Because she was beginning to be able to support herself, we started a new tradition of strapping her into a jogging stroller for family walks each night. Macs and Lolly would run ahead with Cody, playing tag and balancing on curbs, while Avery and I followed behind slowly. I had made a habit of talking to Avery about everything since she was a newborn. Even when I wasn't sure that she could hear me (because I wasn't sure that she would ever be able to hear anything), I would talk to her. And even during the times when I absolutely knew that she couldn't hear me because she was unconscious, I talked on, desperate for her to know that someone was always with her. If she couldn't experience much of the world, I would tell her all about it. So we walked (or rather, I walked and she reclined), and I narrated every detail of the scene for her. She would often babble something unintelligible and then cough, needing her trach to be suctioned. We would pause for the removal of secretions from her airway and then continue on our adventure.

Because her little life had largely been spent inside the sterile walls of a hospital, Avery was an eager observer of the world. She was bright and engaged, and I hoped that meant she also would be intelligent. Her brain had suffered so much trauma and showed so much damage in various ways that I knew learning might be very hard for her. Words might be hard for her. She might have been hearing me, but I couldn't be sure that she was understanding anything I said.

*That's OK, girl*, I promised her in my heart. *We'll work as hard as we have to. I'll homeschool you, and we can do everything at your pace for as long as it takes. We have the rest of your life for this.*

My other thought, as we passed by a row of houses all boasting numerous brightly colored azalea bushes, was that I had no idea how much of the scene before us Avery could actually see. The optic nerves in both of her eyes had been "burned up"—the terminology her ophthalmologist had used to describe what had happened deep behind her retinas. Usually a shade of orange, Avery's optic nerves were a crisp white, and there was no way of knowing how extensively that might impact her vision. We were warned that she might be missing certain fields of vision entirely. She might also struggle to discern colors. I silently mourned all that my daughter might be missing from the glorious pictures we encountered on our walks that spring, but on we walked and on I talked.

The spring before had been so painful. Our family had been ripped apart, and I had been given a front-row seat to the ghastly suffering of my infant and others that had left lasting impacts on my soul. And yet we had survived. God had taken our hands and led our family through the darkest times we had ever known together. Remembering His faithfulness in that season gave me renewed hope as we trudged on. He hadn't left us then, and He wouldn't leave us now. Even if Avery's vision deteriorated, He would be faithful. Even if her brain had been damaged beyond repair, He would uphold us with His mighty hand. He had preserved Avery for a purpose and given her a future. The fact that it wouldn't look like the future I had always envisioned for her didn't mean it wasn't going to be the perfect path for her.

*You are good and faithful, and You always do what is right*, I prayed. My mounting anxiety calmed, and gratefulness swelled in my heart. I was reminded of a passage from Matthew 6 as we walked among the sights and sounds of spring on those cool evenings. "See how the flowers of the field grow. They do not toil or spin. Yet I tell you that not even Solomon in all his splendor was dressed like one of these. If this is how God clothes the grass of the field, which is here today and tomorrow is thrown into the fire, will He not much more clothe you—you of little faith?"

Oh, me of little faith. God had been so good to me, and yet I was still learning and growing in my faith. I realized I would never reach a final faith peak on this earth. I would be slowly moving toward Him until He took me home. I felt like I was moving at a pretty steady pace, but little did I know that He was going to turn up the heat again in the future.

Little did I know that I still had such a long way to go.

# Chapter 27

My phone started ringing. Blocked number.

*Must be the hospital*, I thought, anxious to hear the news we were anticipating. We had repeated Avery's sleep study a few days earlier—six months after her second birthday—and were looking for data about her ventilator settings (she had been on a ventilator for over a year and a half, since a month before her Chiari decompression surgery). Even now, twice a year, Cody and I sleep in the children's hospital's version of a hotel room, watching for apnea progress or regression. We had only ever seen serious, unexplainable regression, so I was anticipating nothing different from the news that day.

"Hello, Mrs. Apperson, this is Dr. So-And-So, Avery's pulmonologist, calling from the children's hospital with the results of her sleep study," he chirped happily.

"Oh, hello, Justin," I almost responded, amused, as I thought of the doctor on the other side of the phone, a petite man with sharp features who was finishing up his fellowship in pediatric pulmonology at the specialty clinic that oversaw Avery's care. One of the social workers attached to the airway clinic had told me that most of the other mothers mentioned his resemblance to Justin Timberlake and frequently asked for him to be the fellow on their children's cases.

I didn't see the resemblance much, nor did I particularly care (possibly because I've never been one to drool over Justin Timberlake), nor did I have any interest in requesting a doctor to practice on my baby based on his looks. Frankly, I liked Avery's pulmonologist because he was obviously smart and very professional.

"Yes, thanks for calling. How'd she do?" I asked, no longer steeling myself for bad news. I didn't become emotional about Avery's ventilator or tracheostomy anymore. Both of those implements were our new normal—no longer just new—so my heart didn't need the protection it once had. Also, we had recently received such positive results from Avery's swallow study that I was still riding that high, refusing to be dragged under by whatever this young doctor had to say.

The premature fusion of Avery's skull bones set off a chain reaction of structural havoc in all nearby areas—including, but not limited to, her nasal passages. They were so small that the tiniest medical scope could not visualize what the base of her nose, the choana, looked like. We theorized that her choana was always mostly blocked by bone—a condition known as choanal stenosis (or "atresia" if the passages are blocked completely), which prevented her from eating as others do.

There were many neurological or environmental reasons for what occurred next, so I can't say for sure what triggered it, but Avery developed a severe oral aversion. Despite all my efforts, she militantly denied any attention to her face, gagging and retching if I so much as brushed her cheek. I practiced every therapy and technique to desensitize her, but nothing worked, and she vomited so routinely that I backed off the oral therapy to give her stomach a rest. This did not change how much she vomited, however, which was upward of ten times per day. I can only liken this experience to having a child with norovirus, every day, for over two years.

All of that trauma had left Avery with significant muscle weakness in her face and mouth, and her burgeoning speaking abilities were being hampered by poor tongue awareness and placement. But after our cranial vault remodeling surgery in April 2017, and six months before the call from Avery's pulmonologist about her ventilator, she began to make serious strides. First, after she had recovered from the major skull surgery, her vomiting dramatically decreased almost overnight—likely due to the fact that her brain finally had a little more "room to breathe"—room that it desperately needed. It seemed that the surgery had also unofficially helped decompress her Chiari malformation even more, which was an unforeseen but welcome side effect. Avery began to show interest in eating by mouth and would even accept small tastes or licks of food. I started to give her a few bites of yogurt each day, though very sparingly. We had never conducted a proper swallow study on her, so I couldn't be sure of where the food could be traveling after each bite.

Aspiration—in which food or drink travels into the lungs rather than the stomach—is very common in children with tracheostomies and those suffering from almost any neurological condition, so swallowing safely is of the utmost importance. Aspiration can lead to a host of serious problems.

Because of Avery's newfound interest in food and her placement in the high-risk category for aspiration, we needed a swallow study—a test during which a child drinks barium while a series of X-rays are taken to see where the food goes. Avery's first swallow study in 2016 showed trace aspiration after every other bite with every texture or thickness of food or drink. I wasn't surprised or terribly upset by this result, since she hadn't had much experience with food and likely hadn't built up the stamina to consistently swallow well. During her first study, we were not able to try liquids through a straw because she was averse to straws. I was advised to still feed her once or twice a day, but to limit the volume of food. I was to use food as therapy and not so much for nutrition.

In September 2017, the week before the sleep study (about which the pulmonologist was now calling me), we repeated Avery's swallow study. She had been begging to try different foods and eating multiple times a day, so I was anxious to see if I could begin increasing volume and frequency of oral feeds in order to limit how often we were feeding her through her G-tube. I was also interested in how she would handle liquids since she had unexpectedly asked for a cup of water a month before and proceeded to drink from a straw all on her own.

I was blown away by what we found.

Avery showed no signs of aspiration with any texture or consistency. Thin, undoctored juice flowed seamlessly from her mouth to her stomach without residue slipping into her trachea. Shockingly, Avery was able to protect her airway from both food and drink. We were given full clearance to let her eat as much or as often as she would like, supplementing with tube feeds for whatever nutrition she was missing at the end of the day. We were even allowed to give her any drink that she wanted in whichever type of cup she preferred.

I cried happy tears.

I had assumed I would be thickening fluids and measuring ounces of food for years to come, but Avery had decided she was ready to experience a bit of normalcy and began scooting around the house with a mixture of apple juice and water in a sippy cup with a straw. The fact that I could purchase the cup from Target was new territory. In the past, all of Avery's cups and spoons had been ordered from a website for orally challenged children. The cup that she most easily managed now was made for average children without special needs.

I excitedly shared the news with the readers of my blog. "We are now in the stage of weaning Avery from her G-tube. I can't believe I even get to type those words. I'm so grateful and surprised by the progress she's made after making absolutely no progress in the feeding department for two whole years. This is also good news regarding Avery's brain. A brain or, more specifically, a brainstem under great stress, would not allow a child to coordinate sucking and swallowing safely, or biting and swallowing safely, so this means that Avery's brain is doing well—which is, of course, the best news I could ask for. A brain that's improving is a brain that may outgrow its central apnea and may, one day, outgrow its need for a ventilator. Holding onto hope about that last one."

I was indeed holding on to hope about that last one, but very loosely, so I was completely unprepared for what came next as I waited for the pulmonologist to share his news.

"She did really well during this last sleep study. It looks like her central sleep apnea has improved considerably, and we feel like it is safe for her to come off of the ventilator," Dr. "Timberlake" told me.

*Wait, what?*

I was at a loss. "Come off the ventilator?" I asked incredulously.

"Yeah, her last study showed an AHI (number of apneaic events per hour) of twenty-two, but this study showed that she's down to four episodes an hour, which is great. She doesn't need the vent anymore, and we can start looking at capping and removing her trach in the future."

I felt like my mind was going to explode. We had just learned that one day Avery would be able have her G-tube removed, and now we were hearing that the tracheostomy and ventilator would not be permanent either.

*For the love of God, everything really is going to be fine after all. She really is going to be a regular kid. Holy crap, we're doing it!*

"Holy—" I added a cuss word. (Sorry again, Jesus.) "I seriously cannot believe it. That's really great. Thank you."

We hung up. Dr. Timberlake headed back to his work, and I sat on the couch with all my dreams coming true, too stunned to know who to call first to share my good news with. I figured it out, but Cody didn't answer, and then my mom didn't answer, so I texted my dad. Looking back, it seems appropriate that Avery's favorite person in the world learned my favorite news first.

"You call Poppa?" Avery asked as I spoke with him, her face lighting up, her words slightly enigmatic.

"Yes, baby, I'm talking to Poppa," I responded with tears in my eyes.

The trach, the ventilator, and the G-tube were going to be Avery's "before", and now, by the wonderful, beautiful, occasionally awful grace of God, she would have an "after." And in that moment, night began to fade away, and the dawn began to creep in.

# Chapter 28

I had been a single mother for a couple of years when my brother-in-law presented a handsome stranger to me after church one evening. "This is Cody. He has been dying to meet you."

I was casually dating a very nice fellow long-distance, so I politely shook hands with the dark-haired man with broad, tight shoulders. "Nice to meet you," I said coolly, determined not to give him any ideas.

I had heard about this Cody before. A year earlier, my brother-in-law had been deployed and was Skyping with my sister. I waved "hello" to him from the background, and he called out, "Hey, my buddy, Cody, wants to marry you! He saw your picture on my Facebook."

"Whatever!" I called back, still bitter from my history of rotten relationships. I was sure this Cody would be like all the others.

As we shook hands for the first time, Cody didn't say anything, but the amused smile and twinkle in his eye bothered me. I could almost sense him teasing me.

*We're going to end up together. It's only a matter of time.*

His eyes crinkled even more, and two dimples appeared on his cheeks. I turned crisply on my heel and walked off, determined to not give this confident stranger another thought, but it was no use. A month later, I was unattached, and Cody and I met after church again. This time, I let my guard down a little. I learned that we had been attending the same church for years and even crossed paths on occasion. Since joining the army, he had been stationed at Fort Bragg, where I was born and raised. Other than deployments, he'd lived mere miles away from me for six years.

My family had a tradition of eating dinner together at our favorite Mexican restaurant after church, so my sister and brother-in-law invited Cody to join us that night. We were not-so-subtly seated next to each other. Everyone at the table joined hands to pray together over our meal, and when I turned to let go of Cody's hand, he delayed in releasing mine. I looked at him, surprised and a little annoyed, and he gave me another dimpled smile.

*OK.*

I raised my eyebrows at him and laughed a little. *He is so freaking cocky. And quiet. Very, very quiet.*

Cody did not say much that night, but he accepted the invitation to join us for dinner after church for several more weeks in a row. He rarely spoke up or ventured his opinion—unless it was to contradict mine, which I found both maddening and endearing, all at once. Mostly, he sat quietly and thoughtfully. Occasionally, I would catch him watching me, and he would flash his dimples. I realized this was a man of few words, and I began to wonder what he was thinking behind that mischievous smile. I was curious and began to rethink my initial conclusion that he was arrogant.

After a few weeks of dinners, Cody asked my brother-in-law for my number, and I agreed to let him have it. Cody waited a day to text, and when he did, it was short and sweet. He asked if he could call me. When he phoned, I could tell that he was incredibly nervous, and for him to be speaking his mind, I knew he must have been very serious about what he wanted to say.

"I'll be out of town this week, but, uh, when I come back, uh, will you, uh, have dinner with me?" He stumbled over his words, and I had to try really hard to keep from laughing at the fact that this American hero, one of the most accomplished soldiers in the world, was struggling to summon the pluck to ask me out.

"Yeah, sure," I said casually, not wanting to let on that I could hear the nerves in his voice.

"Great. Bye." He hung up so quickly that I took the phone from my ear and stared at it for a moment.

*OK. Man, I've never met anyone like this guy.*

The thought both intrigued and worried me. He was so nice. And quiet. And he clearly thought I was worth pursuing, though I couldn't understand why.

*That's alright. You'll have him running soon enough.*

I frowned at the thought and worried at the rising hopefulness that was blooming in my heart. I didn't really want Cody to run. I wanted to know him a little more. I wanted to hear what was in that mind of his, but I knew that sharing any future with him would also mean sharing my past. I resolved to tell him everything sooner rather than later. No surprises, no sucker-punches. He could decide whether he wanted anything to do with me after that. I also didn't want to wait too late and get too attached if he was going to change his mind about me.

We texted a few times over the next week. He sent me a picture of the sunrise over Big Sur, California, with the rugged Santa Lucia Mountains overlooking the Pacific Ocean. "Not as beautiful as you," was his caption, and I smiled. I was charmed by his simple directness. He wasn't flowery with his words, and he flirted sparingly, but I could feel that he was sincere about getting to know me.

We went on our first date, and Cody made it very clear that he wanted the relationship to move in a meaningful direction. I told him there were things he needed to know about me first. We sat on the couch in my downstairs apartment after Macson had fallen asleep, and I told him about my past—about how used up and dangerous I was. I expected him to have some type of overtly negative response, but in true Cody fashion, he didn't say a word. He simply put his arm around my shoulder and pulled me close to him. I wondered if he was saying goodbye, but after a moment of silence, I looked up at him and he smiled. "I've already heard all of that before. Your brother-in-law told me before we met."

I stared at him in disbelief for a few seconds. He had known everything about me the entire time. He had known, and he had pursued me anyway. He had heard, considered, and made the decision that I was worth the risk.

Just like Jesus. He had known my faults and failures and died for me anyway. I was beginning to learn that real love didn't keep tally marks for mistakes. Love didn't think in terms of "used" and "damaged." Love knew all and still decided that I was worth the trouble.

# Chapter 29

For the next ten months, Cody and I were mostly inseparable. He was still quiet and thoughtful, but occasionally he would show his heart in delightfully endearing ways. We had barely been dating a week when I said something especially funny. He broke out in a thunderous laugh and pulled me into a tight embrace. "I think I love you," he said sincerely. I just smiled.

*We'll see.*

We attended church together each week and made dinner for each other at our respective houses several times a week. I couldn't believe how kind and generous he was. My car broke down in our first week of dating, and it needed more than a jumpstart to get started again. I called my younger brother Stephen first and asked him to give Macson and me a ride home while I figured out how to get my car to the auto shop for repair. When I spoke with Cody later that afternoon, he was offended that I hadn't called him first. "I'm your boyfriend! You should be asking me for help," he chided. "I want to help."

The thought made me bristle at first because I was so intent on not needing or depending on any man ever again, but then he blew me out of the water with what he did next. My car had stopped working outside of Macson's preschool and had yet to be towed. I knew that Cody was a handy man, but I had no idea how handy. I learned quickly.

A few hours after he learned of my car troubles and where I had left the vehicle, he drove up to my house in my previously broken car.

"What did you do?" I asked incredulously.

"Your starter was broken, so I replaced it." He shrugged. His hands were stained and dark from working with greasy car parts.

"You replaced it? Just like that?" I asked in disbelief. None of the guys I had dated knew their way around a car like that.

"Just like that," he said and smiled one of those dimply smiles.

He wouldn't let me pay him back for the part that he had replaced or anything else, for that matter. When we took my car anywhere, if I stopped for gas, he would race to beat me to the pump and fill my tank, hip checking me out of the way if I tried to insert my debit card to pay for it.

*Gosh, he's wonderful*, I marveled.

On the weekends, we would spend every waking minute together. We would meet for breakfast, and then Cody and Macs would watch cartoons together for several hours, sitting side by side on the couch, while I devoured book after book on the opposite couch. We made elaborate dinners, set off fireworks for holidays (even the holidays that don't usually involve fireworks, but such is life when you're dating an army engineer), and frequented movie theaters till far past Macson's bedtime to see the latest kid movie and eat massive amounts of popcorn.

We had been dating for a month when Cody asked that Macson and I join him on a trip to his childhood home in Ohio to meet his family. They were kind and welcoming, and I couldn't help but fall for Cody a little more after seeing him in his natural environment. He came alive in the hills of Ohio, looking like a little kid playing with his brothers. He talked more and relaxed more, and I knew things were getting serious as we drove home when the weekend was over. Macson slept cozily in his car seat, and I looked over at the delightfully muscled man in the driver's seat. I could see us eventually making a family together, yet I was still afraid.

I tried breaking up with Cody on several occasions with the excuse that we were "going different places"—that our futures were incompatible—but he was unmoved by my attempts and never took my relationship reservations too seriously. It was as though he knew exactly where we were going to end up and that I would catch up when I was ready.

Ten months after our first date, Cody and I married in front of our two families. He had received orders to deploy with his unit shortly before he proposed, so we were engaged for twenty-one days before our wedding, marrying quickly enough to have a little bit of time together before he flew to the other side of the world.

We spent a perfect month together before we were separated for eight, but not before his baby had taken up residence in my belly—our first daughter. I had desperately wanted another baby and was ecstatic to share the news with Cody over Skype, since he was already deployed when I learned that our family would be expanding. He was thrilled as well, and I couldn't believe that everything in my life was working out so sweetly after so many years of pain.

This strong, steady man had chosen to love me and my baby boy. Soon he would love our newest baby girl as well. He hadn't been afraid to stand beside me as I slayed my dragons and faced my demons. He was gentle and kind as I struggled to settle into the wife role that I so resented once before. He was patient with me as we learned how to parent together in our blended family. He was a rock that I could count on, the rock on which our family was built.

His strength would be tested in the days to come, and I would learn exactly what he was made of. We didn't know it, but God had a fire waiting for us. And I could not always see it at the time, but the heat was turning my husband into gold.

# Chapter 30

With a failed teenage marriage under my belt, I was intimately aware of the studies that predicted that most marriages would fail in a crisis—like the one in which Cody and I now found ourselves.

Before Avery's birth, our marriage had its share of bumps like any other, but it was relatively smooth. Our biggest disagreements were always about parenting, since I had been a single parent with sole custody for years before we married, and co-parenting with Cody tapped into my fearful, controlling tendencies. Ultimately, we were the average family. I stayed at home with our two children, homemaking and home educating. Cody was the breadwinner, working and training for hours each day, often leaving the house for work while it was still dark. I considered my responsibilities a much lighter burden to carry, so pampering and catering to his wishes was my pleasure. Still feeling the sting of regret from having been a terrible wife on my first attempt, I worked with vigor to make my family happy. At the time, motherhood was a breeze, our home was sweetly decorated and peaceful, and my husband generously encouraged my many artistic interests, such as

purchasing a fancy camera or buying special pens for practicing cal-
ligraphy. (I'm still awful at it.) We were happy, and life was truly sweet.

I didn't mind picking up the dirty laundry scattered in Cody's
hurried wake, and it didn't occur to me to resent him for taking time
for himself on the weekends, as he often did. We purchased a new
house, we took the children on vacation, and we settled into our new
family life.

Our marital cracks began as tiny chips before Avery entered the
world. Cody refused to believe her prenatal diagnosis and frequently
verbalized that he absolutely could not have a child with a disability.
I had felt for eight months that something was very wrong with my
pregnancy, so the confirmation of what I had feared unleashed great
sadness in my soul. I cried myself to sleep a couple of times following
Avery's diagnosis after devouring any and all research about bicoronal
craniosynostosis that I could find, but I couldn't share my findings or
concerns with Cody because he refused to hear them.

The fractures became breaks in the days and months after our
severely disabled baby was born. I was in love with and committed to
this new little life that needed me from the moment I set eyes on her
broken body and swollen face, but Cody's disposition toward her took
much longer to warm up. His obvious disappointment sliced at my
heart, and I had to actively, continuously choose not to be offended
when he would vocalize it. He needed to vent, but my weary, burdened
soul warred with rage and "mother bear" protection over my new
daughter and against my husband and teammate. The enemy of my
soul, bent on death and destruction, was thrilled with this new position—Cody on one side and me on the other, with Avery securely
tucked behind me as though her own father were the opposition. It's
easier to lie to, steal from, and destroy a family when it's in crisis.

We lived apart for most of Avery's first year, me in the ICU
with her and Cody at home with our older children. We had easily
navigated a long-distance relationship several times before, but the
added stress of our new life was the perfect breeding ground for

misunderstandings and division. We often disagreed about treatment courses. One of us would push for a tracheostomy to solve Avery's airway issues (Cody was first), but the other wouldn't be ready. Then our opinions would reverse.

When Avery was able to spend time at home, I assumed every ounce of responsibility for her care. Her supplies, appointments, packing and unpacking for appointments. I knew every medication and dosage, and I charted the exact schedule for administering each one. My compulsivity often paid off, but at great cost to my soul.

I was pumping breastmilk for Avery to receive via feeding tube around the clock and pouring the rest of my energy into the all-consuming, never-ending list of tasks necessary to sustain such a medically fragile and complicated life. Because my grip on Avery was so iron-tight, Cody let me take all of the weight upon myself. I lived and breathed medicine. I researched and debated with her caregivers as I became as much of an expert on her conditions as I could without a medical degree. I prided myself on being the most equipped to provide her care. I *had* to be the best. Unfortunately, I did not interpret Cody's backseat role as his recognizing and appreciating my newfound obsession with—and easy understanding of—this new frontier, but as disinterest in Avery as a whole.

His clothes left on the floor began to feel like a slap in the face. Because I envied his job and felt as though going to work would have been a welcome reprieve, I began doing less and less for him as my responsibilities elsewhere piled up. After all, my work was much harder, I rationalized.

We began to escape—me into my research and reading medical journals for calm and comfort, while Cody sought refuge outdoors, gardening and building furniture to de-stress.

We drifted apart. There were no curse words, no punches thrown, and no outrageous behavior, but we were losing it. I needed him for financial support and health insurance, and he needed me to care for the children and our home. We entered into a never-spoken agreement to be civil roommates.

I wish I had some great story, some dramatic moment to point to the eureka that changed everything, but I don't. Change is rarely dramatic. It rarely happens all at once. Most often, change is tiny steps in the right direction. Sometimes it may seem as though we are taking tiny steps right in place, but change is happening as long as we keep moving. I wasn't asking Cody to meet my emotional needs (since neither of us was very much in touch with our own emotional needs), so I clung to Jesus like He was all I had, because at the end of the day, He really is all I have *ever* had. The funny thing about Jesus is that He never lets you stay the same in close proximity to Him, and because He's more interested in our calling than our comfort, He gently and lovingly showed me my own selfishness and pride. To this day, I'm still selfish and proud, but because I learned to rely on Him more than ever before, His transformative work in my life was accelerated like never before.

I took steps toward Cody. I picked up the dirty clothes like always, but with less malice. I knew that at the end of my days, when I stood before my Maker and was held accountable for my life and marriage, there would not be an allowance for how nice or supportive my husband was or wasn't. The question would be if I gave everything that I had to do the absolute best job that I could with what I was given. I knew that God wasn't concerned with who was giving more in my marriage, but with who was willing to give everything—with no regard for the effort of the other party.

I resolved to honor even when I was not feeling honored; to love when I was not feeling loved; to be present, even if the other party seemed to be chronically escaping. I gave Cody space to grieve the way he needed to grieve. If he needed to spend every minute of every weekend outside, decompressing and de-stressing from our crazy life, then that was exactly where I wanted him to be.

Cody began to take more and more responsibility with Avery, venturing opinions that he had always had but rarely felt the need to articulate because I was doing enough talking for the both of us. In turn, I learned to be quiet more often (a work in progress). When

Macson unexpectedly needed heart surgery, Cody took excellent care of Avery and Lolly at home by himself for a week. I didn't have to worry about my bizarrely complicated system because Cody had it under control. He was more than capable—if I would get out of his way. His instincts were phenomenal. He was steady under pressure and mastered tricky trach changes when the thought of them still made me feel queasy.

Something that surprised me years later was how largely unaware he was of what I perceived as marital stress. What I interpreted as agonizing distance between us he remembers as, "Oh, that? I used to get a lot of projects done back then." I thought we were drifting apart, but, apparently, I was the only one drifting. He felt that we were as connected as we had always been, or at least as connected as we needed to be during that tough season. He thought that I was just busy and had a lot on my mind. I had felt as though he was taking steps away from me, but, in truth, I was the only one shutting down. I was tapping into old coping measures that weren't necessary because my husband was and always has been on my side. The outworking of his grief was a trigger that made me feel as though he was going to abandon or betray me. But his behavior was not a sign of his lack of commitment to me; it was grief. He was withdrawing *to* his projects to process, not withdrawing *from* me. My faulty perception of his intention—as author and research professor Brené Brown calls it, "the story in my head"—was not an accurate picture, and I am deeply saddened that I spent those years of our marriage feeling cut off from my husband unnecessarily.

Day after day, I moved toward him, and day after day, we became a more cohesive team. Sometimes I'm shocked at how natural our dance has become. Our life is immensely different than we ever would have imagined, but I believe my appreciation for my husband is much greater than it would have been if I hadn't watched him walk through fire with me like he has. He never left our family, and he never betrayed us. He tirelessly provided and prayed. He always allowed me to be angry and wrong, and he still chose me every day. A fact that will stick with me forever is that even during the worst of our times after Avery was born, Cody came home immediately after work every day. He never lingered or pretended to run errands to stay away. Though no one could have blamed him for taking some time to himself after work for a little breather, he never did. He always came home.

Perception in crisis is a strange thing. You see and experience life through a filter of adrenaline and fatigue, believing that what you're feeling and seeing is inherently true, but only in hindsight can you fully appreciate history the way it truly was. Cody and I were grieving. We were disappointed. We had felt loss. Life was excruciating in that season, but Jesus was using the fire to mold our relationship. The heat made us pliable, and He was smoothing edges and bringing unity while we were unaware. The heat slowly brought a closeness that I never could have dreamed of, and in hindsight, it revealed a track record of mutual commitment to our marriage that we both valued above all else. Life was hard, but we stayed. There were times of significant physical and emotional distance while I lived in the hospital with Avery, but we kept choosing each other. Even in all the hurt and misunderstanding, I still knew that he was the only person in the world that I could have suffered alongside. I knew the weight of our family was safe on his shoulders. I knew that Cody loved Jesus more than he loved us, and that he would serve us as though he was serving his Savior as long as he still had breath in his lungs.

No one has loved me more like Jesus than Cody. He is everything I ever could have wanted in a husband, and I feel so undeserving of his love and so impossibly grateful to be the recipient of it.

I believe the key to surviving that season of our marriage was not thinking of myself more, but thinking of myself less. It was easy to see all the ways in which I was hurting or being hurt, but to turn my gaze around and consider the ways that my husband could be better supported and loved helped the hurt fade into the background. I can't change Cody or control him. That is God's job, not mine. I can only offer the best of my love for as long as I'm blessed to love him.

Recently, I asked Cody why he was so certain we should marry all those years ago. "I just knew," he said with a shrug. "You were always meant to be mine."

*Meant to be.* Three little words with so much significance. Our family was meant to be. Avery was meant to be. Our collective story— the plan that God wrote for us in all His awful, glorious grace—was meant to be.

# Chapter 31

"If I treat her like she's sick, she's going to act like she's sick."
I have repeated this phrase over and over in my head a thousand times since Avery's birth. Almost every aspect of my motherhood has had to adjust since meeting my unique baby girl. Every inclination that came so naturally to me—the rhythms that I relied on to parent Macson and Lolly—did not serve me once Avery was born. I couldn't feed her the way I knew to feed babies. I could not comfort her the way I had comforted my older children. There were new considerations to be acknowledged for dressing, sleeping, bathing, medicating, and playing. This new baby did not even breathe the way my older children had, and when it came to rearing her or disciplining her, I didn't have the first inclination of where to start.

Over bland hospital food in an equally bleak hospital cafeteria, another mother of two medically fragile children had shared my conundrum. How do I create and enforce boundaries for a baby whose neurological status is so unknown, whose physical makeup is so tenuous? And what will happen if I don't?

The other mother shared with me a story she'd heard about a pediatric oncologist who warned a mother of the dangers of enabling her son, who was newly diagnosed with leukemia.

"If you let him run all over you; if you give him everything he wants; if you remove all of his boundaries; if you let him speak to you however he pleases—if he makes it, you will have made an uncontrollable brat. And in that way, you will lose him."

On a significantly smaller scale, I had crossed this bridge at the time of Macson's surgery to repair the coarctation of his aorta. The pediatric cardiothoracic surgeon had stressed to me that thoracotomies were among the most painful surgeries a person can endure, and indeed, Macson's recovery was nothing short of agony.

He was sedated and on life support for a full day after the procedure, and I had stayed by his side praying and strategizing. I knew that once he woke up, I could show no weakness. I knew that I could not cry or show fear on my face, or he would panic. I knew he needed to be able to express how much he was struggling, and my job was to always remain calm. I knew he would need compassion and some serious tough love. I knew that all the time he was spending on a ventilator could allow fluid to build in his lungs, and he would need to cough and exercise them in order to avoid developing pneumonia. I knew, with great sadness, that the nature of his procedure would make those very acts—specific and crucial to his recovery—excruciating. His side had been slit the length of my palm between two ribs, which had been wrenched apart with metal prongs to give the surgeon access to Macson's descending aorta and aortic arch. The narrowed section of aorta had been resected, and the remaining ends had been sewn together. A tube had been placed through his chest cavity to allow any residual fluid to drain after the surgery, and he would wake with several feet of rubber tubing attached to his body and pink liquid seeping into a bag on the floor.

Upon extubation three days later, my usually mild-mannered, respectful son was reduced to a skeletal waif who was writhing in his bed, begging for relief, and begging to go home. He became aggressive and angry, lashing out at nurses in the cardiac ICU. His chest tube made breathing excruciating, and he cried out whenever his positioning was adjusted. He needed to begin moving as soon as possible to hasten his recovery time and force his lungs and muscles to regain their strength and full function, but he tearfully pleaded, gasping and sobbing, to be left alone.

I could not acquiesce.

The same day that he was removed from life support, I assisted him as he stood from his hospital bed and shuffled to a recliner, propped with pillows. He ate popsicles and Goldfish as the sun from the expansive window streamed across his ghostly, pale face.

Later that day, we made the trek back to his bed amid his protests and complaints. I had to hide my eyes often as they welled with tears at the pain it caused me to push him out of his comfort zone—in the kind of pain I wasn't even sure I could endure. I told him repeatedly, "I love you, and since I love you, I must make you do this."

Days later, he was recovering well but still deeply resented the nurses' interference. He could tolerate slow laps around the halls and hourly breathing treatments, but even the mention of assessing his chest tube brought on an outburst.

"LEAVE ME ALONE!" he had growled at one nurse who was poking around the dressing that covered the ghastly incision on his back. On several occasions earlier in his recovery, I had allowed him to be a little mouthy, likening his behavior to that of a woman in labor. You don't blame a woman in transition for crying out or yelling at a nurse to "get back." But once I knew his pain was well-controlled and he was rapidly approaching discharge, I stepped in.

"I understand that you're in pain, but you are not going to sass this nice lady who is trying to help you," I said with no emotion. I kept my voice quiet yet firm, and I moved very close to his surprised face so I could look him straight in the eye. "You will apologize to her right now."

I smiled slightly at the end so he would know that I wasn't angry. Boundaries aren't about anger; they're about right and wrong.

Macson stared at me for a moment to ascertain if I was serious and if this line in the sand would remain, and then he slowly turned to apologize to the nurse.

He never spoke another aggressive word for the remainder of that hospital admission. He never developed pneumonia either, even though an X-ray immediately after extubation days earlier had shown a significant buildup of fluid in his lungs. Despite all of his protests, we walked the halls. Despite his tears, we completed breathing treatments again and again. And even though it hurt him and it broke my heart to see him suffer, we actively faced the pain that was necessary for his healing.

I knew that loving him in this context meant that I could not enable him. Loving him meant making him do hard things—even when they hurt. Loving him meant making him treat others around him with respect—even when he was exhausted and worn. Even now, loving Avery looks much the same.

I cannot run every time she cries. I must push her outside her comfort zone every single day in order to facilitate her development. I don't rescue her during therapy sessions. When she crawls into a tight spot, I cannot scoop her out. I have to stay back and watch from the sidelines, verbalizing support as she learns to solve the problems at hand.

This approach has not always gone over well. Before she could speak, she would protest by looking away and frowning when she didn't want to participate in her strengthening exercises. As she grew older, she began to verbalize her frustration. First in little sentences like "No wanna!" Then they changed to "I too tired!" Then she learned to say, "I don't want to do this anymore"—with the cutest, stormiest scowl, folding her arms and plopping down on the floor with her back turned to her physical therapist.

"I know, baby, but you can do it. You're the toughest girl I know," I would say with a smile.

"You always say that," she would respond begrudgingly, returning to her task.

My heart yearns to protect her and shield her from any and all necessary pain, but my brain knows that's not how life works. I know that enabling and coddling her will strip her of her independence and slow her growth. I know that enabling is disabling. One day, baby Avery will be an adult Avery who must know how to solve problems and do hard things. Adult Avery will often have to look pain right in its hideous face and not shy away. She will have to know that her heart is as strong as it is beautiful and that she does not need me to make things all right. Avery will slay her own dragons, and many dragons there may be.

God allows our dragons. He has already called us to be brave and courageous. He has already put the tenacity to face our struggles deep in our hearts, and He equips us to do the work, slay the beasts, and win the victory that is already ours. He doesn't rush in and scoop us out of our pain. He allows us to sit in it and slowly be changed by it.

# Chapter 32

*P*ain. My teenage years and young adulthood were wrought by it. Before Cody, before Avery, before I believed that all the pain had a purpose, before I believed that it was actually for my good, there was this: I said "I do" when I absolutely, undoubtedly did not. I lied, believing that if I went along, did what was expected of me, denied myself for long enough, kept myself quiet and small, and avoided rocking the boat with all the strength I could muster that I could keep everyone happy and life would eventually be fine. But that is just not how things work.

After marrying the first time, I quickly became pregnant. I suffered from a severe form of morning sickness called hyperemesis gravidarum, which left me hospitalized and initiated several bouts of pre-term labor. By eight weeks, I had lost over ten pounds, and by the end of my pregnancy, I had only gained twelve of those pounds back—seven of which were Macson's birth weight. To say that I was in a very bad physical and emotional state would be an understatement.

In retrospect, I believe my body was telling the truth of my life even as I tried to hide it. I was betraying myself, and my body was angry about it, so it decided to revolt. My relationship woes largely ceased to concern me because my focus turned to survival. The entire first trimester was spent tinkering with doses of anti-nausea medication. My doctor tried several drug cocktails but with very little success. During one experiment, Reglan, which was a popular anti-emetic drug at the time and one that I have mentioned before, seemed to curb the nausea enough—but it induced thoughts of suicide. I was advised to stop taking the medicine immediately and go to the obstetrician's office for an IV infusion in preparation for the onslaught of vomiting that would ensue. We finally settled on the drug Zoran for enough nausea relief to survive at home, which I managed narrowly. I had to set an alarm to wake up during the night to take the drug so that I would never let the dosage lapse. Any break in nausea coverage would result in severe dehydration from constant vomiting. I expended all my mental and emotional energy staying "on top" of my medication.

My relationship with my son's father seemed to balance out a bit during that period, partially due to my inability to be quite as insufferable as usual and because I largely couldn't care or even be hurt by whatever behavior he was participating in or who he might be wooing behind my back. I was also immensely grateful for any help he could give me that would ease a bit of my physical exhaustion, and that sense of gratitude curbed some of the venom in my soul toward him.

I still simmered in incredible rage, but carrying my baby thawed out my frozen heart just enough for me to take to motherhood like I never imagined I would. The day Macson was born, I became an exclusive breastfeeding, baby-wearing, full-time caretaker to the most glorious human I had ever known. He became my reason to live when the familiar thoughts of the ultimate escape plagued me.

I suffered from postpartum anxiety (though I had no idea at the time) that presented itself as an irrational, frantic fear of harm coming to my baby. I didn't eat much, I stopped sleeping, and I was terrified to be alone with my thoughts. I began to binge-watch episodes of *Law & Order: SVU* at an excessive rate. It seemed to me that watching every episode of that show would somehow give me a "leg up" on keeping my son safe from predators. But watching the show brought back to my mind those parts of my past that I never knew could be classified as sexual abuse.

I thought rape only occurred in dark alleys, perpetrated by strangers. I did not know that you could know or maybe even love your assailant. I did not know that ages were very important in differentiating between normal sexual experiences and abuse. I did not know that sexual assaults didn't always involve screaming and crying. Sometimes those assaults involved my pushing roaming hands away until they found me again. Sometimes the assaults lasted mere seconds. Sometimes I was complicit. Sometimes I gave up fighting, resigned to endure. But every time, the assaults occurred while I was a child.

Watching *SVU*, I learned that there was much I had not known. The waves of knowing crashed over me, and the memory and realization of my own lost innocence came back in choking nightmares. I finally understood my hate. I finally understood my distrust of people. What I had sought so long to suppress reared its ugly head, and I grew to blame God for what He had allowed.

*You didn't protect me. How can I trust You to protect my son? If You are so good, how could You let things like this happen?*

I thought perhaps God had betrayed me. (Maybe religion had betrayed me.) I did not yet know that I was simply betraying myself. I tried to pretend with all the grit I could muster, but it was no use. The fake began to fade away, and my heart turned away from my Savior, though not before I sought help once more. I went to counseling.

I vaguely (what a mistake to be vague) shared details of my abuse that should have warranted more questions but instead were met with blank stares and Bible verses. I began to resent those Bible verses and the people who shared them. I felt as though the verses were shared to condone the abuse that had occurred and to silence me. I also discovered that no amount of going to church or attending Bible college could fix me. Pretending was getting me nowhere, and because I had truly believed that pretending would be my ticket out of pain, it seemed the only option left was rebellion. The problem with rebellion is that it gets you about as far as lying does: it gets you stuck in a pit of crap.

My family still had little idea about the extent of what was really happening with me. They knew I was going to counseling and appeared to be troubled or grappling with my faith or life—or both—but they had absolutely no idea about the kinds of things I was sharing with my counselors or how dangerously desperate I was becoming. I had silently been in a crisis of faith for several years before I decided to turn my back on the God I thought I knew. I couldn't take another Bible verse.

*I've tried Your Way, and it didn't work. It's time to do things MY way.*

"My way" consisted of lighting a match and tossing it on the pretend life that I had built—and boy, did it ever burn. I did the worst thing I could possibly think to do: I had an affair that began and ended as quickly as a scrap of paper that has been set ablaze turns to ash. I told on myself—confessing with a shockingly eerie calm, icy and dispassionate. When the people I had hurt cried, I simply stared straight ahead. I was so good at betraying myself that apparently I was also an expert on betraying everyone else. I was so numb to the sting of my own self-betrayal that I was numb to the heartbreak of others' as well.

My life imploded, but my marriage dragged on. We attempted counseling half-heartedly for several months until I knew that no matter what anyone else thought or believed, the answer was staring plainly in my face—though it took me a full year to finally make it. I knew lots of people would have a lot of things to say about Christians getting divorced (and they did), but I also knew that I would rather take my chances with God than Christians on this one, even if He and I weren't on the best of terms.

I moved back into my parents' house with my eighteen-month-old baby. I had no friends, limited support, no career, and no reputation worth hanging on to. That's when I knew I had nothing left to gain by hiding anymore. Behind the fake, behind the facade, was just the same five-year-old girl, scared to death and too afraid to honestly look at herself in the mirror for fear that she would see used, damaged goods. I was a woman whose main talent was running away from the truth.

There are details about this time of my life that I could share that would make your skin crawl. There are details I could tell you that might elicit some empathy toward me and make my decisions more understandable, but those details are not meant for this book. Instead, what I would like you to know is that I walked into that marriage sinfully and left it during a season that was just as sinful. My decisions were my own, and regardless of the circumstances leading up to my marriage's demise, I hurt many people through my actions.

The move back home to live with my parents again was suggested by a dear family friend who began by asking me to share my story as honestly and plainly as I could. I had recently destroyed my life and was seeking help for my floundering marriage. I had no real intention of staying married (though I had no idea how to navigate a divorce), but I felt that seeking advice was at least the right thing to do. I told my dad's oldest friend my story, and his eyes grew wide. He had been a source of support for many other families besides my own, and his approach to rehabilitating my wreckage was both firm and compassionate. He untangled the timeline of my story and affirmed that what I had suspected to be abuse during my teen years was indeed abuse, in all its subversive, insidious "glory." He felt that I wouldn't be able to seek healing unless I could return to the safety of my childhood home, away from what had always been a toxic, war-zone-like environment.

So my marriage was put on hold. I packed Macson's things with my own and left the house where I had carried him—his first home. We never returned.

I spent the next year in therapy with counselors who specialized in helping those who have been sexually abused to navigate the wreckage of my life and with a Christian family counselor to navigate the separation from Macson's dad. I also began to dismantle my version of religion, which was more about self-betrayal than truth. I slowly learned that Jesus didn't really care how hard I worked to keep everyone around me happy if I accomplished it by lying. I had to go back to the "drawing board." Who was God? What did He want with me? And what did He have to stay about the whole mess? I had my own questions, but one day, He would ask one of me.

*Meg, do you trust Me?*

# Chapter 33

Divorce is a horrible thing. Sometimes it is a necessary thing and should be handled with the utmost care, but I believe it is still horrible each and every time.

My crisis of faith was further propagated by the resistance to divorce that some in my circle felt and readily shared with me. The fact that they clung to the idea that marriage should be preserved at all cost, regardless of the reasons behind the separation, stunned me. I felt conflicted, knowing the impression I had formed about divorce growing up—about how much God hated it, how sinful it was, how painful it is for children caught in the middle (I believe this to be absolutely true), and about how there could be no happy future for those who picked such an unfortunate end to their relationship.

But I also could not believe in a God who would value an institution over the safety of His children. I had known women married to men who consumed porn so prolifically that they were unable to be satisfied with a physical woman. Those women had stayed in the relationship because some well-meaning Christians had quoted verses about

God hating divorce. Wasn't there a verse in the Bible for those women too? To set them free, to give them hope?

I had known women who were emotionally or physically brutalized alongside their children but chose to stay because we are called to forgive. What message did their staying send to their children? How many generations were to be impacted by staying silent in the face of atrocities?

I had known women married to men with perverted and illegal sexual proclivities who stayed longer than necessary because they weren't sure their husbands' improprieties met the standards of adultery mentioned in the Bible. They weren't sure they were able to get a divorce that would be sanctioned by their Christian community, so they endured. What about Matthew 18:6 and its warning to those who prey on children?

"If anyone causes one of these little ones—those who believe in me—to stumble, it would be better for them to have a large millstone hung around their neck and to be drowned in the depths of the sea." God hates divorce, but He says it would be better for that type of man to drown in the sea.

God created marriage, and I believe He feels strongly about it, but I think we've attributed a lot of different ideas about marriage to God that perhaps He didn't actually intend. God *does* hate divorce, but I believe that He hates abuse of all kinds just as much. God *does* call us to forgive, but He never says we have to continue living with a dangerous abuser. Personally, I believe that God is more interested in delivering those who are being abused and oppressed in marriage than He is about saving all marriages.

Through my wrestlings and untanglings, I came to know the God of the universe who transcends systems of beliefs and denominations. I learned more and more about His nature as I feverishly searched the Scriptures for His thoughts on the ending of relationships. More and more, I began to see the Who behind the words of the Book I'd read for so long. Maybe the Bible verses weren't the problem; maybe unwise application was the issue.

I had known God as a child, but now He was beckoning to me as an adult.

✳      ✳      ✳

At twenty years old, after tearing my life apart piece by piece, I finally shared my secrets about all the years of hidden abuse. I finally blew the whistle, years and years too late. The truth would be the only thing that could possibly set me free.

My family was shocked. A criminal investigation was initiated, and I learned that I was not the only person in my circle who had been victimized. I learned about a predator's grooming process. I learned that I had been his "type" and that others had been his type as well. My world changed forever, and the justice system began its work.

I went to counseling again—no longer desperate, but completely broken. Because my family now knew the depths of my trauma, I was sent to an accredited professional counselor who did not quote a single Bible verse to me. She, the first of many, began the daunting work of untangling me as a person. At first, I was unable to fully grasp what had been done to me all those years. I couldn't call it "abuse." Not out loud. There was a part of me that still believed my relationships had been normal. My experience had been that romantic relationships and abuse could coexist. I realized now why I had always run from nice men: their offering of love lacked abuse, so it didn't really seem like love to me.

Every part of me had been shattered, and it was among all those cracks that the real healing light of Jesus began to break through. I will be the first to tell you that my healing and restoration were not a linear process. It took years for me to relearn how to live. I had to practice making decisions based on reality and not feelings of fear. I had to learn how to have relationships as a powerful adult—not as a victim. I had to learn how to discover and enforce my own boundaries. I had to learn how to fight against the deeply ingrained fear of disapproval that had driven so much of my life. I had to learn to trust my instincts. I had to begin to untangle the web of lies I had believed about God. I had to decide if I truly believed at all.

And though I was unaware, God had been waiting with open arms in sovereign anticipation. He had been waiting for me to break and surrender myself into His hands. He had been waiting to shine His light on my life, and then He would be asking for my idols.

The road back to Him was bumpy and full of misgivings. I didn't know it at the time, but we were building a track record—a memory bank full of the grace and goodness of God, so that when the time came to surrender, I would be ready. He was proving Himself trustworthy to me even in the years that felt like desert and famine. He had led me from captivity—the jail I had created for myself, built from the bricks of abuse, self-betrayal, and lies—and right into the wilderness.

The years that followed were a slow, steady journey toward healing and wholeness. Jesus was taking my broken mess and putting me back together. And when I thought He was done, I learned that He was just getting started. I still needed to learn how to trust Him with my idols— the idol of holding tightly to the ones I love and the idol of approval. The first, He'd ask me to surrender by nearly taking my children from this world and by allowing me to believe that Cody might abandon our family. The second, He asked me to crucify, slowly, more and more each day.

I know something is wrong, but I'm afraid to be demanding. *Be demanding anyway.*

The doctors might think I'm difficult and aggressive. *Make a scene anyway.*

The nurse might think I'm rude. *Confront anyway.*

I might be wrong and look foolish. *Risk your appearance anyway.*

People might react to the truth. *Speak it anyway.*

Sharing our story might open us up to criticism. *Share anyway.*

Maybe no one will read it. *Write it anyway.*

If I wanted Avery to live in the world the way I hoped she would—on her own terms, regardless of whether people accepted or included her and regardless of whether they approved of her face or were put off by her imperfections—I had to live that way as well. I couldn't hide. I couldn't stay quiet to keep everyone comfortable. I couldn't be afraid.

I had to trust.

# Chapter 34

Before I met Avery, I had no idea that holidays could be cruel. I didn't know that the happiest time of the year could make me feel like an outsider in a room full of people—people laughing uproariously at an inside joke that I could not understand because I no longer spoke the language of cheer and bliss and holiday happiness. My mind had been stained by the suffering that I had seen during those months of living in the hospital.

The smell of the fifth floor of the children's hospital—the pulmonary and oncology ward—would not fade away. I could not forget the hallways where children with airway problems lived next door to children whose bodies were overcome with cancer. I could not forget the little boy who escaped his room every day to stand outside Avery's door. The nurses always knew where to find him. He was so interested in her new trach. I wondered if he would live to see his next birthday.

As a child, holidays were magical. Both sets of my grandparents lived within driving distance, so I could wake to one beautiful Christmas tree, holiday pancake breakfast, and mountain of presents on Christmas morning and then wake to a different tree, Southern holiday breakfast (complete with eggs, bacon, biscuits, and home-made jams galore), and a different pile of presents the following morning. Pure heaven.

As an adult, holidays took on a different tone—less blissful but more fulfilling—until the year that Avery was born. Thanksgiving was the first holiday to survive, and I was unprepared for how my grief had changed my ability to celebrate. I tried very hard to be normal or to at least pretend to be normal, but it was no use. My parents and siblings were together in the mountains on a trip that had been planned long before Avery had entered the world and changed all our lives, and my nuclear family was unable to join. We were living in high-alert, high-stress mode, shut in our home, nursing a near-comatose Avery back to life and easing Macson back into normal activity after his surgery. Part of me was sad to miss the trip, but another part of me couldn't grasp the point of celebrating anything. I threw together a special meal for my children because I really didn't want to be responsible for them telling a therapist later in life about the year their mom banned holidays and how that had hurt their precious hearts, but I was not prepared to celebrate. My heart was stunned, weary, and broken.

Thanksgiving would never be the same. Nothing would ever be the same. Would Avery live to see more Thanksgivings? Would she ever sit in a seat and feed herself with a fork? Would she ever cook a Thanksgiving pie or bring a boyfriend home to spend the holidays with her family for the first time? Would Macson's heart continue to deteriorate? Would his aorta dissect in the middle of dinner?

My grief was smothering, and my marriage was smoldering. Cody stormed out of the house and stayed away for several hours that day. I don't remember the reason, but I'm positive it wasn't important. It never was. He could be set off by anything and disappear without a word, and the kids and I would carry on until he calmed down and decided to return. And I was unbothered because nothing could bother me, I decided. I was a robot, and he was a tornado. Grief does crazy things.

As I write this, I am not grieving anymore, and my marriage is not unraveling anymore. Holidays are fun and enjoyable, but I cannot forget those painful years or unsee the agony I beheld in the lives of others walking down similar paths. Each year, I think of them in the midst of the cheer and festivities and excess.

I think of my cousin Sara and her baby girl, Mina—a baby with beautiful brown hair and dark almond eyes who was born with adrenal cancer and died days later, betrayed by her body as it developed in the safest place on Earth. I think of Sara and her family frequently, but especially around the holidays. I think of Mina's forever empty seat at the table. I think of who she would be today.

I think of my friend Rebecca, whose first daughter, Abrianna, was born perfect, but still—stolen by the mistakes of a medical provider flying too close to the sun.

I think of other mothers bringing sick and broken children home from the hospital for the first or possibly the last time, too scared and exhausted to bake a pie and too overwhelmed by the future to consider hanging ornaments they would eventually have to take down.

I think of two boys and a widow in my town who will experience their first holidays without their dad and husband, murdered for the sake of freedom half a world away. I think of a folded flag and an empty uniform, and I wonder how they make it through any day without him, let alone Thanksgiving or Christmas.

And since having Avery, I've begun to wonder if someone who passed me at the grocery store that year, scurrying to buy potatoes and cranberry sauce, would have been able to tell that I was drowning. I wonder how many people are cooking and decorating and buying and scurrying and dying inside this year, too afraid to raise their hand in the middle of the frantic celebrating to say, "I am not OK! Someone, please see that I am not OK."

So I walk a little slower in the grocery store now, and I watch my fellow shoppers a little more closely, and I judge strangers and friends a lot less harshly. Because while I am again able to converse in the language of holidays, I remember the year that I couldn't—and I never want to forget.

Grieving gives you a new lens through which to see the world. I think grief gives us Jesus's eyes. I think, for all our pain and suffering, the gift that is always left in grief's wake is compassion—the ability to see the agony of the universe and the will to ease it in whatever way we can with whatever is left in our hands.

# Chapter 35

There were months, perhaps years even, when our family commuted to the children's hospital several times a week to meet with Avery's specialists. Cody's career stalled, since he could only accept positions of minimal responsibility that allowed him ample time off to tend to his family. Besides doctors' appointments, we were largely confined to our house, unable to travel or frequent restaurants that might expose Avery's delicate lungs to maladies stronger than her fragile body could bear. I blogged about these times, desperate to feel some sort of connection to the outside world—a world beyond the medical field and Avery's protective bubble.

That desperation eventually waned as I found the social media world a jarring and frequently unwelcome place for images of Avery. I began to receive graphic and violent comments and messages about what should be done to Avery and what should be done to me for allowing her to live. I began to think that perhaps seeking connection was exposing Avery—and my other children—to eyes that did not deserve to behold them. I slowly backed away from the blogging world, archived and removed many images from my social media sites, and began to partake in those forums less and less. I had already chronicled years of Avery's journey on my blog, and I felt that the families who needed to hear our story would be satisfied with what I had already shared about our experiences. I was not interested in simply sharing for sharing's sake; I only wanted to share content that added to people's lives. Once I felt that I no longer had something to add, I stopped.

As I limited my interactions with the world, my focus turned inward in a richer way. Instead of viewing my home as a canvas for my social media posts, I began to treat it as my haven from that world. I began by decluttering, simplifying my family's existence and responsibilities. I became disciplined about meal planning and grocery shopping, preparing for the days when Avery's appointments would leave me too exhausted or short on time to make a nutritious meal for my family. Instead of ordering out, an expensive and unnecessary strain on our increasingly limited resources, I was prepared with meals that could be made quickly or simply pulled from the freezer to heat for my family—meals I had already made on the weekend, when no appointments could be scheduled.

By reducing the number of belongings I had to manage, I reduced the amount of time I spent managing those things—usually miscellaneous items that we never used. Instead of scrolling through apps, I turned to books for mental stimulation. Instead of treating this season of our lives as a time to endure—a bump to get over—I began considering it our new normal. And in order for it to be "normal," I had to accept it as such. I couldn't be surprised or thrown off by the stresses; I had to face them head on, plan for them, and treat them as though the stressors were certainties. Doctors' appointments would go long. Traffic would be bad. Avery would continue to vomit throughout the day, no matter how I wished otherwise. Nurses would call in sick. Medical equipment would be faulty. I had to plan for all these eventualities every time; that way, when the ridiculous and inconvenient happened, I was prepared with a backup plan. I wouldn't be caught without a way to suction Avery. I wouldn't be late or caught off my guard. I became light on my feet and quick in my head. Avery's circumstances required nothing less.

When we originally chose a tracheostomy for Avery, the doctors told us she would likely only need it for two years at most. The years dragged on, and Avery was no closer to decannulation, but our ease and familiarity with her care continued to improve. Cody and I stopped expecting that Avery would improve and simply began acting as though her limitations would be permanent.

Though our family made great strides toward health as a unit, I was still feeling weak and grief-stricken. I chided myself for feeling so disconnected. After all, I had a living child—several, in fact. In seasons when I had watched other children die, I had promised myself that I would never take a living child for granted—and yet I did not feel much joy. Life had normalized as much as it possibly could, and still the darkness of what I had seen and lived through clung to the depths of my soul. Our family was doing well, and I had implemented many positive changes, but good exterior circumstances can only do so much for a heart in turmoil.

Little did I know that God was about to use the writings of an unlikely character to initiate the process of breaking me open and shaking me up. It was time to let the sadness go.

*          *          *

It did not happen all at once. I can't even tell you when it started, but gradually, I stopped grieving. I realized this fact after a season that had been especially dark. I had become obsessed with discerning how grief impacted my thoughts and actions. Then I became preoccupied with accepting the reality of death and sitting with the truth that eventually everyone I had ever loved would die. My children. My husband. My parents. Life would be fatal for all of us, no matter what.

I'm not sure why accepting this fact brought me peace, but it did. I read Joan Didion's memoirs regarding the sudden death of her husband

and, later, her only child—a daughter who became critically ill in the prime of her life. Didion's writings were not from the perspective of a fellow believer, but they were a healing salve for my heart all the same. Didion did not seem to have the same need to find the silver lining in her suffering as I had. She saw the pain for what it was, no more and no less. She acknowledged it without brushing it away and without searching for any deeper meaning. Pain was pain, loss was loss, and life went on. And sometimes as life was moving on, it felt hollow and meaningless, and that was all a part of the process—an important place to get comfortable, a place to call home for a time.

I became aware that my constant grasping for any sign of positive purpose had been prolonging my grieving process. I needed to accept the pain for what it was, not preach to myself about all the good that was coming from it. I had to sit with the fact that some pain will never go away on this side of Heaven. I had to come to grips with it, and then let it go.

So I stopped posting on social media for a while, and I stopped looking for the bright side every time pain pricked my heart. I let myself hurt. I held space for myself in the darkness, and I started to let the hurt run its final course. Jesus was there all along, and He wasn't whispering sweet nothings in my ear, telling me that everything was rosy and full of rainbows. He was sitting with me in the darkness and holding my hand as I let it all go. And slowly but surely, life stopped feeling quite as hard. The darkness was fading, and the sunshine was breaking through—not because I had forced myself to see sunshine, but because I had been willing to sit in the darkness without running from it. I had learned to accept that maybe there were times where the sky was simply dark, and the only thing that brought out the stars was having Jesus by my side. Maybe the sky would stay dark forever, or maybe one day there would be sun again, but as long as I had Jesus, everything would eventually be made right. Maybe not on Earth, but certainly in Heaven.

The year 2018 dawned. Avery was making great progress, and meeting her needs had become second nature to me. Activities that had seemed forever out of reach fell within the realm of possibility for us again.

For years, Cody and I had attended church separately. He went to a service on Sunday morning while I kept Avery at home, and then I attended a service on Thursday evening while he took a shift with her. As she began to need fewer and fewer interventions, we started going to church together again with her little body seated snugly between us. She listened intently and sat quietly, in awe of the sea of people and captivated by hearing her Poppa speak.

We started to travel more. I felt rested and motivated to work on the book I had been writing for several years. I thought we had reached a nice "ending" to the story that I had been working on, but I had no idea of what was going to happen next.

# Chapter 36

At the end of January that year, my older sister stopped by my house to introduce her new baby to my children. Avery and Lolly were obsessed with their newest cousin. As Avery admired him, she turned to me and said, "I want a baby in your tummy too."

I laughed and told her, "Absolutely not!" While I had considered the idea of having another baby, I couldn't get past the feeling that it wouldn't be wise to try. I wanted to be able to focus all of my attention on Avery, and I was afraid that another baby might slow down the progress we were making. More than that, I had a lot of unanswered questions about Avery's genes and what had caused her mutation, so having another child felt like a risk that was too selfish to take.

Two weeks later, I was up before the sun as usual. When I poured a cup of coffee into my favorite mug, the smell made my stomach turn. I stopped in my tracks, and my heart began to race. I forced myself to drink the coffee, trying to prove that the aversion I felt was a fluke. The next morning, I poured another cup of coffee and again felt repulsed. By the afternoon, I had to make myself a second lunch because I felt ravenously hungry.

*There's literally no way*, I thought to myself as I crawled into bed earlier than usual that night. I was exhausted. We weren't trying to have another baby. In fact, quite the opposite. I knew Cody would be thrilled if I "fell" pregnant, but I couldn't even wrap my brain around the possibility of having another child.

A few more days passed and the signs became ever clearer. I realized I wouldn't be able to ignore them forever, but each day I talked myself out of purchasing the necessary test. On Valentine's Day 2018, I finally summoned the courage, but I still believed there was a different cause for my unusual symptoms. I dropped Lolly off at preschool and drove to the nearest grocery store in absolute terror. On the way to the checkout counter, I clutched the box I was carrying under my arm as if it were full of illegal drugs. Honestly, the significance of its contents was much scarier to me than illegal drugs, and I could barely look the cashier in the eye while she rang it up.

I almost choked when she asked me, "What are you hoping for? Positive or negative?" I shrugged sheepishly. I was embarrassed to be a woman in her late twenties buying this little box unexpectedly. It meant that something had happened that I had not intended.

*I'm a grown-up. I know how to avoid this kind of thing*, I thought, annoyed with myself.

Minutes later, I took the test I thought I would never take again, and immediately, one extra blue line appeared and confirmed what I had been too scared to verbalize to a single soul: I was pregnant. A clump of cells had taken up residence in my abdomen, and they were multiplying whether I was ready or not. My legs went limp and I crumbled to the bathroom floor.

*Oh, God—what have we done? I can't do this to another child. I can't possibly doom them to a life of suffering because they share my suspicious genes. How could this have happened? Why did You allow this?*

The words I felt that I heard in my heart shook me to my core and put me firmly in my place.

*Do you think I'm limited by something as small as your genes? Do children grow in their mothers' wombs without My knitting expertise? Who do you think you are that you believe your genes have the final say?*

My fear and sense of genetic responsibility collided with my theology in that moment as I had to make a choice about how I would walk through the next months.

I believed that everything about Avery's life had been divinely orchestrated by God, and yet my pride had elevated my genetic importance in the situation and had perpetuated the worry that something inherently wrong in my biology had betrayed my baby girl. The paradox was crushing.

If I had learned anything in the years since Avery's birth, it was that God did not deal in accidents. He was never surprised. In the worst pain of my life, He was the Master weaving a beautiful tapestry. Some threads were ugly and wrought with pain, but they always intersected with hopeful redemption.

*You're right. You are the Master Creator. You are not limited by my humanity. You make ways where there are no foreseeable ways. You've never left me; You've never failed me. Your will be done.*

# Chapter 37

Before my embarrassment in the grocery store that day, our life had become so settled. The days passed smoothly and easily. We were able to travel more often and visited Avery's specialists at the children's hospital infrequently. She rarely underwent procedures. Her shunt seemed to be functioning well, and her cognitive function seemed to be good. She was frequently sick during flu seasons, but she spent all other times largely well. She had been in speech therapy and physical therapy for years, and we were really beginning to see the fruit of all her hard work. She began to communicate as well as her older siblings and make exciting strides in all other areas of development.

One of our main concerns had always been Avery's supremely delayed gross motor skills. Her progress was always slow and incremental. Around her second birthday, she started to crawl, but she did not make much additional headway for another year. But as she grew, her momentum increased, and she began to make improvements. When she was three, Avery mastered drinking through a straw and walking with assistance. She began to need less medical equipment and learned how to do basic things such as brushing her hair and teeth.

As Avery's care became less stressful and her progress more dramatic, my health improved. I was sleeping well and had increased energy. I had a sense that we had all hit our sweet spot as a family. During those peaceful times, I would fleetingly long to have another baby, but my twisted reasoning always prevailed.

*Your genes could be dangerous.*

*Your genes are the only link between Macson and Avery—and look at all they've been through so far.*

*It would be irresponsible to have another child.*

*How guilty would you feel if you make that one sick too?*

*Your body is not fit to carry children.*

I believed these sentences with all my heart, so whenever another woman announced a healthy pregnancy, my insides twisted a little. I was excited for her and yet grieved for myself. It was as though for all my faith, a corner of my heart rejected the grace that God had so lovingly soaked my life in for years. I just didn't want to release the idea that the corruption in my genes was responsible for Avery's suffering and possibly Macson's, though no doctor I consulted felt that Macson's heart had a defective genetic component. I still wanted to believe I had the tiniest bit of control, even if it meant my body was unfit. I still needed someone to blame—and as usual, that someone was me.

With that extra blue line on that pregnancy test, the line that shocked and terrified me, God was calling that lie out into the light. The lie that my body was defective. He was making me confront, once and for all, my utter lack of control and utter dependence on Him in all things. It was my final crushing.

\*       \*       \*

The first trimester of my fourth pregnancy was very stressful. Macson had picked up a virus from school that seemed mild. One Saturday morning, just as he seemed to be completely well, he woke up with bright pink cheeks that looked as though he had been slapped, and I groaned. Those distinctive pink cheeks meant he had contracted fifth disease, and now I—and the baby I was carrying—had been exposed. Fifth disease is a common childhood illness that usually presents mildly in children and healthy adults. It is only dangerous for those with compromised immune systems—and it may cause complications for pregnant women.

I was still in denial about being pregnant, so I had yet to make contact with my regular clinic for prenatal care, but I dragged myself to the emergency room for a blood test to check whether this exposure could hurt my developing baby. Thankfully, the blood test confirmed that I had an immunity to parvovirus B19. After my fifth disease scare, I experienced bleeding on multiple occasions. I suffered from severe dehydration from nausea and vomiting that caused an electrolyte imbalance and induced strange heart symptoms. I spent several afternoons in the emergency room being monitored for episodes of arrhythmia that lasted for over twelve hours. My heart function was fine, but my blood pressure was erratic, and I couldn't seem to get on top of my hydration.

In previous pregnancies, I had used an anti-emetic drug called Zofran to control my nausea (to some extent), but I had resolved to do without it during this pregnancy. Because of this, dehydration wreaked havoc on my entire system as I struggled to consume enough fluids. I have always been prone to prenatal depression, and this pregnancy was no different. Fear, intensified by all-day sickness, made those months feel dark.

When I finally made an appointment to see my usual obstetrician, which was further into my pregnancy than normal because of the denial, I was expecting to have a few normal visits before being referred to a specialist to make sure my new baby was forming well. I tried to check in for my first appointment in the regular obstetric clinic, but the receptionist told me briskly, "Oh no, we can't see you down here yet because of your history. You'll have to go upstairs to the Maternal Fetal Medicine clinic to meet with the specialists first."

The sentence sent shivers down my spine. I had not prepared myself to go back to that office where Avery had first been diagnosed with craniosynostosis before her birth. I had not considered how I might react because I thought I surely had more time to process how I might feel before I had to walk the long, white hallways and take the empty elevator to the office that monitored the high-risk women and sick or compromised babies.

It was my first time in the perinatologist's office since Avery's birth. The same doctor who had caught her abnormalities on ultrasound was about to check on the new baby budding in my abdomen, and all I could do was tremble. Sitting in the waiting room brought memories of those weeks before Avery's birth flooding into my mind as my pulse quickened and my stomach tightened. It had never occurred to me that there was still trauma from that time clinging to the deep recesses of my soul. I realized that if I didn't calm my central nervous system, I would have a panic attack. I started consciously slowing my breath and purposely relaxing each muscle as I waited for my name to be called. I closed my eyes and waited to feel my heart rate return to normal.

*You brought me here, Lord. I never would have chosen this on my own. I'm afraid, but You're used to that from me. I'm ready to do this all over again if You're with me.*

"Margaret Apperson?"

I looked up to meet the gaze of the friendly nurse who remembered my case from four years before. I steadied myself and followed her to the familiar dark room that could again radically change my life, but as soon as I saw my newest son's body on the ultrasound screen, I felt peace. The panic began to melt away, and I found myself enjoying the ultrasound. Cody and I didn't know the baby's gender and weren't convinced that we wanted to find out, but within a few seconds of seeing the images displayed on the ultrasound screen, I had my answer.

"Oh gosh, that's a boy," I said, and I laughed.

"I knew I wasn't going to be able to hide that from you!" the nurse replied, chuckling as well.

After the specialist confirmed that our new baby was growing well, I was referred back to my normal obstetrician with only occasional specialty appointments. We saw a pediatric cardiologist for another ultrasound to check on the baby's heart, but each appointment was another confirmation of health. Despite all my worries and fear, our baby boy was growing perfectly.

# Chapter 38

My pregnancy with baby Ryan (we decided to give him Cody's middle name) progressed well. Because the pace of our lives had slowed so sweetly, I brought Macson home from the private school he was attending to resume the home education we'd been pursuing before Avery was born. Avery had been so healthy that our private-duty nursing hours were drastically cut, and she could no longer have a day nurse. My last trimester was spent working out new routines because homeschooling and also doing all of Avery's daytime care was new for me. It was glorious, and I pushed my anxiety about having another baby momentarily out of my mind.

I loved not having a nurse in the house. Our home instantly felt cozier than it had in years. When Cody and I weren't bonding over our various shared interests, we were completing home improvement projects. Or really, he was completing home improvement projects that I designed while I cheered him on from the couch.

Summer turned to fall, and our family had never been closer, but as we neared Ryan's due date, the panic that I felt over giving birth steadily crept back in. Flashbacks of Avery's birth and all the moments afterward flooded my mind and gave me nightmares. As each night closed in around me, the contractions I was beginning to have would increase in intensity, and I would lie on my left side with my knees curled up toward my chest willing my body to make it stop.

*Please, Lord, I'm not ready. I don't think I can do this.*

My second trimester and most of my third had almost convinced me that I would feel strong through the end of my pregnancy, but I was unnerved by how increasingly rattled I felt. God had never let me down before, and yet I felt panic at the thought of what could happen next. I knew the devastation that could accompany the birth of a baby, and I knew it could happen again. I knew Jesus wouldn't leave me alone no matter what happened, but my body felt bone-weary and almost too tired to choose peace. It had been easier to trust Him when my body felt strong, but now as I unraveled, I was worried I would lose Him in the darkness.

*Lord, I feel weak and scared. Please tell me that everything is going to be OK.*

I heard no answer.

*       *       *

The midwife laid the baby on my chest. His eyes were open, but he wasn't crying. He lay still. Terror began to rise up inside me, and suddenly I was in another room down the hall, and the baby that had fallen silent wasn't my new baby, but Avery.

As quickly as I slipped away, my thoughts jerked back into reality. My mind was spinning wildly, and I kept asking, "Why isn't he crying? Why isn't he crying?" I began to pull back from him in order to see his face more clearly, allowing him to slide from my chest to my stomach. My pitch raised slightly, "Why isn't he crying? Is he OK?" The midwife slid the baby back up on to my chest and lowered herself to my level.

"He's OK. Just look at him. He isn't in distress. He's content. His eyes are open. He's breathing easily."

I felt embarrassed for my distress and kept apologizing, "You're right. I'm sorry. He's OK, he's OK." She smiled reassuringly and said that she could understand why I would be feeling afraid. I smiled back nervously.

*Great, is this how I'm going to be from now on? Nervous and jumpy? How embarrassing.*

I tried to regain some composure.

*I am the mom of a medically fragile child. I've been handling stressful situations without panicking for years, so why am I panicking now?* I was annoyed with myself and my weakness, and I tried to think of other things.

My labor had gone well. This baby had been born in record time and with minimal effort from me. Because our insurance had cut Avery's overnight nursing care hours completely, we hadn't had a nurse to watch her at home when the time came. She was in the delivery room with me throughout my entire labor, watching Netflix on my phone as her brother was born. She was a helpful distraction. I've always had the ability to tolerate a lot of pain without showing my discomfort on the outside, but I was especially motived to stay silent and controlled during my labor for Avery's sake. Between contractions, we would talk and smile at each other, and during contractions I would kneel next to my hospital bed and roll my neck, letting my head fall side to side. I barely climbed back onto the bed in time for her brother to slide out.

It was so fast and unexpected, and I was concentrating so hard on not showing my pain that the end of my labor felt almost violent, as though the pain would rip my body in half. I think perhaps hiding pain gives it much more power than it really holds. Holding my groans inside my body had kept the discomfort trapped, and the agony that resulted was more painful than the other labors I had experienced.

Ryan Apperson was born ten years and one day after the birth of my oldest son, Macson, signaling the end of a decade that had broken me, built me, tormented me, tested me, destroyed me, and finally delivered me. And through it all, God had been faithful. He had been more than faithful; He had been good.

But this new season had to be about more than remembrance. I couldn't merely rest on my track record with God. I had to learn to take hold of His mercies that are new each day. I could not rely on the old mercies. I had to find Him in all things even as my mind betrayed me. I had to trust Him to sustain me even as the whole world went dark.

# Chapter 39

Ryan was beautiful and healthy. I knew I should be relieved, but instead I felt dread. Cody had taken Avery home for the night, and again I sat in a hospital room with a fresh child. I tried to take solace in the bundled baby boy in my arms.

I marveled at his thick brown hair and kissed his sweet face over and over. He had that intoxicating newborn smell, and yet something didn't feel right. *I* didn't feel right. I tried to act normal, but my mind began its treachery. When a male nurse took Ryan from my room unexpectedly without showing me his hospital badge or even mentioning why he was taking him, I thought I might be in serious trouble. This was the baby that no one was going to take from me—and yet, suddenly, he was gone. My room was empty like it had been the night Avery was born. My body was swollen and heavy, my arms aching and empty, just like before.

My heart began to race, and I felt a phantom pressure on my chest that restricted my breathing. My mind conjured up worst-case scenarios of someone stealing my baby in the dead of night from his nursery, and I sat in the corner of my room with my back pressed up against the wall, gasping for breath. In an effort not to lose complete control, I closed my eyes and focused on relaxing every part of my body from my feet to my furrowed brows.

*Just breathe slowly. In and out. Let your nervous system regulate everything else.*

The panic passed, but I knew this episode was merely the beginning. I hated being right so often. My baby was eventually returned, but the fear had not subsided—nor would it for months to come.

Ryan's exit from the birth canal was so rapid that his lungs were still very wet for his first few days of life. He hadn't been adequately "squeezed" during my precipitous pushing stage, one nurse joked. Because of this, he would frequently vomit and choke on the fluid emerging from his lungs. I felt sheer and utter terror each time. I held him at an angle that I had learned from holding Avery through so many terrible nights that would allow him to clear his lungs more quickly, and I mentally prepared for the moment I might need to intervene. I had watched Avery gag and choke and gasp for breath for years; I couldn't bear to watch the same take place with this tiny new life.

I felt helpless and enraged at my helplessness. With Avery, I could change her trach or suction her airway to help her breath more easily. With Ryan, I just had to wait patiently for him to clear his airway himself. I spent most of his first night holding my breath like I had in the living room with Avery three years before, willing his airway to clear.

On top of the emotional turmoil I was experiencing, I was in physical agony as well. Postpartum contractions had always been a part of my experience and had been very painful before—but in the hours after Ryan's birth, they were the worst ever. Cody had returned from taking Avery home to visit me and had to remove Ryan from my arms so that I could scream into my pillow and curl up into a trembling ball. During the labor and birth, I had been able to maintain my composure, but in the aftermath, the pain was too overwhelming. The pains were worse than my labor contractions, and I could not understand why.

In the tumultuous days after Ryan's birth, I felt that I could count on at least one thing to be easy. I had never struggled to breastfeed before and felt completely seasoned and competent to handle whatever this new baby could throw at me. His latch was great, and we were on a good nursing schedule, but after the second day of nursing, he became extremely agitated. We were discharged from the hospital, but Ryan's disposition did not improve. Though I was nursing him every two hours, he screamed frantically and clawed at me as Avery had done when she couldn't nurse. I wept almost constantly as well, drowning in the memories of everything Avery had lost and how, yet again, I was doing everything I could to help Ryan and still felt helpless.

When he was three days old, we took him back to the hospital for his weight and jaundice check. Though he was spitting up fluids, making it seem as though he was nursing well, he had lost a significant amount of body weight. My body was not producing milk, and Ryan was starving. The doctor instructed me to bring him in for daily weigh-ins to ensure that I was taking adequate care of him. My confidence as a mother vanished once again. I couldn't even *feed* this baby right. I knew my brain was out of sorts, and I could tell it was getting worse. I asked about supplementing with formula. I said that I didn't care about breastfeeding anymore. I had mourned that missing piece of my relationship with Avery, and yet I was prepared to leave it in the past for Ryan as well.

"I just need him to stop crying," I said to Cody through clenched teeth when he seemed surprised by my request for formula. The day that I almost gave up, my milk finally came in. Ryan still screamed much of the day and night (he did this for more than six months), but at least he wasn't crying due to hunger any longer. He quickly regained the weight he had lost, but I continued to ponder what had gone wrong and where my milk had been all that time.

I was entering a new phase of my healing journey that did not feel very much like healing. In patients with severe burns, the healing process is complicated. The dead skin and tissue may need debridement in order to facilitate growth. Debridement is the removal of those damaged tissues through various treatments. Non-surgical debridement methods may take weeks, and the removal of the skin occurs slowly.

Through my pregnancy and postpartum journey with Ryan, God was drawing my old motherhood wounds, gashes, burns, and cuts that occurred after Avery's birth back to the surface. He was lovingly scraping back the scabs and dead skin to allow for new blood flow and mobility. It was not a fast process, but a gradual and shockingly painful method.

He was about to allow every trigger in my soul to be set off.

# Chapter 40

"Sometimes this happens," the doctor said. "Your body appears to have retained a large piece of placenta."

The delay in my milk production, the excruciating postpartum contractions, the hormones that left me raging and depressed, the tingling in my extremities, and breathlessness during any activity were all the product of a postpartum complication that can have deadly effects on the afflicted mother. I was lucky that my body had resolved the issue on its own four weeks after Ryan's birth, but in the interim and subsequent recovery, the significant blood loss was painful and demoralizing.

Ryan was the worst sleeper of all my children and had terrible colic for months. His entire disposition was demanding and aggressive. He was frustrated with nursing. He was frustrated with sleeping. He was frustrated by being a baby. His pediatrician felt certain that he was highly intelligent and merely resented the limitations of being small and immobile. He learned to crawl before he turned five months old, and that curbed some of his screaming, but he remained irritable. I introduced solids earlier than I had with my older children in the hopes that heavier foods would help him feel more satiated. As with any child, he had to learn how to manipulate foods in his mouth through trial and error and the occasional gagging. On top of already feeling off my game, watching Ryan nearly choke was a serious trigger point for me. I would feel helpless and frantic, and often I had to look away from him and use my sense of hearing as a gauge for whether or not he was OK.

*He is coughing productively. Just keep listening for his cough. If he's coughing, he is moving air. If he is moving air, then he will resolve this on his own.*

He never choked badly, and he never needed me to intervene, but I dreaded giving him solid food every day because of that fear. I felt sheer, utter panic each time. I was afraid that he would need me to help him and that I wouldn't be able to save him—just like all the times I had been unable to save Avery from pain. I was triggered by the feeling of helplessness, the feeling that I should be able to stop my baby from struggling, but that was never the design. A baby learns to eat by eating. Either keeping him from solids or rushing to pull the food from his mouth would have kept him from learning how to solve the issue on his own.

I felt triggered by Ryan's constant screaming. It was hard for me to not visualize that something was terribly wrong every time he wailed. When Avery had screamed as a baby, it meant that she was in agonizing pain that needed to be addressed. With Ryan's colic, I had to learn to set him down and walk away or hold him without letting my mind run wild about obscure things that could be ailing him.

At each well-baby visit, his pediatrician would assure me that I had a healthy baby. She was also Avery's doctor, and she knew very well why I struggled to manage my anxiety about something going wrong.

"I feel like one day I'm going to wake up and discover that something has been terribly wrong with him all this time, and I'll be guilty for not helping him sooner," I told her. She understood and checked him carefully, but there was nothing to discover. I had an average baby with colic. The problem was that I had not been the average mom for the last four years. I had become so accustomed to looking for rare problems that it was hard not to look for them even when there was no problem to find.

I have discovered that being the mother to a special-needs child is sometimes like swinging a sword at imaginary opponents. We become so used to fighting for our children that it's hard to know when the fighting has stopped and it's OK to put down our weapons. Ryan had no fight. He just had a bad attitude. I knew my instincts were good, but my anxiety had found a way to be louder in those days.

Avery needed me to fight for her; Ryan needed me to stand back and let him work things out on his own. I had to learn to be able to do both—sometimes simultaneously, and sometimes at different times. I had to learn to mother malleably again, not rigidly and fearfully. I had learned to trust God with my children, but now I had to learn to trust my children to grow and develop at their own pace. I had to learn to stay back and offer support when they needed it with ready hands and a peaceful heart. I had to learn to trust the process of childhood.

Avery needed me to hold her hand through every step of the feeding process. I had to guide her through every aspect of her gross motor development—but when it came to potty-training, she needed me to step back and trust her timing. A process that I thought would be painful and arduous took three effortless days.

Learning to step back and pick my battles brought whimsy back into my motherhood. Breathing through my anxiety and allowing my children to take some of the lead (when appropriate) brought joy back into my mothering style. So many things that seem like issues in parenthood sort themselves out if we'll only have the patience to trust the process.

Ryan learned to walk at eight months old with no help from me. I had been agonizing over Avery's slow walking progress for years, thinking of how unfair it might feel to her to watch her baby brother stand himself up and learn to walk in a day. I worried that she might feel demoralized by how he had surpassed her, but his progress had the opposite effect. Avery and Ryan had been crawling side-by-side for months. Avery was capable of taking steps, but they remained shaky and uncertain. As Ryan transitioned from crawling to walking, Avery did the same. I was shocked. At her physical therapy appointments, Avery's therapist marveled at her quick progress.

"What's gotten into her?" she asked incredulously.

"She's just following her baby brother's lead. He started walking, and it was like Avery decided that walking is all we do around here!" I laughed.

"Sometimes we just need a buddy," she said.

God had provided a buddy for Avery and a catalyst of healing for me. During a year that felt like I was being forced to sit in a scorching fire, God was still at work molding, pruning, and restoring.

"See, I have refined you, though not as silver; I have tested you in the furnace of affliction" (Isaiah 48:10).

His beautiful, awful, amazing grace was at work again, and He gave our family the gift of a gorgeous, healthy baby boy as a bonus.

# Chapter 41

In the years after Avery was born, I had been able to force my body and mind to endure intense activity. But in the year after Ryan was born, I couldn't force anything. I couldn't force happiness or energy. I couldn't force motivation or empathy. I felt dead and numb and disconnected again. It seemed like I was frozen yet burning to death, screaming yet silent, thrashing yet paralyzed. I functioned, but with great effort. Hiding how poorly I felt took even more effort. My thoughts felt disjointed and illogical, yet I couldn't stop them from playing from the same script.

*Your children would be better off with a different mother, and Cody would be happier with a better wife,* bounced back and forth through my skull. I couldn't stop the dark words that taunted me or the frantic speed at which my thoughts raced. Panic would rise from the back of my shoulders, slide up the back of my neck, cover my head, and slam down on the middle of my chest, sucking the air from my lungs.

I knew I didn't feel like myself, and yet what was happening also felt like reality. Like I really was a terrible, unsafe mother. Like I really was an unsatisfactory wife. I wasn't sure how to make it right, so I just nodded in agreement, as though the lies were the truth.

*I am He who sustains you. I have made you, and I will carry you; I will sustain you, and I will rescue you.*

As I continued to read the Bible through that year, God would speak verses to my heart. Through the confusion I felt, little moments of clarity grabbed me through His words.

I read the third chapter of Lamentations and began praying for His compassions that never fail to be available to me every morning.

*You are my portion; therefore I will wait for you.*

Reading the Bible was my source of truth in a time that felt so uncertain. When I had been in darkness before, I had felt God's Presence enveloping me, but in these new days, I had to search to discern it. God was not withholding from me; my capacity to experience Him felt diminished by the battle raging inside my head.

I considered reaching out for help, but it felt selfish and futile. I felt that as long as I could continue to function and pretend that I was fine, I could find my way out of whatever was ailing me.

*It's just hormones,* I told myself over and over, as if explaining the source limited its power over me. I tried to downplay what I was feeling. I tried to say I was merely tired. (I was.) I tried to say that it was just that I had a lot on my plate. (I did.) I tried to tell myself that one day I would feel normal again, but I couldn't quite remember what normal looked or felt like. I had been in various levels of crisis for the past five years. Who was I without a crisis?

I began to search for ways to "go back home," as I called it. I wanted to find and do things that made me feel like the person I had been before I had children, before motherhood and suffering had begun to accumulate layers of coping. I began to reread books that I had loved in the past that had spoken to my heart. I decided to take up running, something I had loved as a teenager.

Running had been the catalyst for recovering from the obsessive, disordered dieting that had occupied so much of my time as a young person. I had no intention of running for anything more than a few minutes, but I ran two miles on my first try. Half a mile into the run, my mind felt sharper than it had in years.

*There's something to this*, I thought excitedly. Fresh blood flooded into my groggy brain, and the world suddenly felt crisp. I felt at home on the pavement with the sun on my face and the fall air filling my lungs. I knew in that moment that I had wasted enough time downplaying my mental and emotional needs. I had denied how poorly I was feeling for too long. By hiding, I was lying all over again. I needed help. Running, reading books—all of my own efforts weren't going to be enough. I needed a professional.

Shortly after Ryan's first birthday, I called the office of the psychologist that I had regularly met with after Avery's birth. She had helped me navigate that stressful period of my life, but it had been a long time since I had seen her. In hindsight, I should have called her as soon as I found out I was pregnant. When I hung up the phone after booking an appointment, I sobbed. The relief of finally seeking treatment for my scrambled thoughts was overwhelming. Only on the other side of the sadness could I see it for how dark and terrible it was. As my thoughts cleared and my mind slowly thawed from its muddied spell, I was shocked by how miserable I had truly felt. For almost a year, I had gone to bed feeling sad and woken from each sleep even sadder. There was no physical crisis at hand, only thoughts darkening my mind.

Denying pain doesn't make it disappear, and trying to tough it out isn't always noble. Seeking help didn't make me weak; it finally made me wise. My pride had kept me in sadness and hopelessness.

Before Avery and Ryan—before even Cody and Lolly, when my life revolved around one small brown-eyed, brown-haired baby boy—I heard a song at a Christian conference in Sydney, Australia, that changed my life forever. A beautiful woman sang a remake of "Blackbird" by the Beatles while a massive screen behind her showed flashes of black feathers. I had come to the conference in rough shape, desperate for some hope. I was nearly divorced after a year-long separation from a relationship that was never meant to work, and I was totally terrified about the next steps. I was about to be divorced—a single *Christian* mother in a religious world that didn't really like the words "divorced" and "Christian" in the same description. I knew that being fully divorced was the right next step, though my therapists, parents, and a handful of others I had trusted with the details of my life were the only people who agreed. And I was scared—so scared to pick up the pieces of the life that had been so shattered by lies and the uncomfortable truth.

But then, as the black feathers flickered across the screen, I realized the song was meant for me. I was broken, with sunken eyes and a pitch-black horizon up ahead, but I felt God whisper to my soul that I would arise and indeed learn to fly. He promised to repay me for the years the locusts had eaten (Joel 2:25). So I returned home, and without telling another soul, I tattooed a black feather on the back of my neck (also meant to be a cover-up tattoo, but that's a story for another book). "Blackbird" and a quote by Emily Dickinson about how "Hope is a thing with feathers that perches in the soul" convinced me that I was called to be like this blackbird, and the song I would sing in the dead of night would be one of hope.

Then Avery came, and I knew that my old version of hope was nothing compared to this new hope, the kind of hope that glows brightly—not in a life of no struggle, but in the heart of one who sees the fight and races toward the pain, determined to overcome because she knows that she doesn't race alone or toward pain that was not already crushed at Calvary. She knows she can trust the One who knits children in wombs, who calls from burning bushes, who calms the storms, who heals the sick, and who calls each of us home at our appointed time.

Again, I felt as though my wings had been clipped, and all I could do was sing out into the night. But as my mind cleared, I felt my metaphorical wings being loosened as they had all those years before. I believe that God could have dispelled my sadness of soul with a single word, and yet He let me stay in it until I was ready to ask for help and search for hope—until He had sufficiently refined me as He saw fit. It was a terribly unpleasant process and a terrifying place to be, but all I can say is that He was kind to me in the midst of it. He was good when Avery almost died, He was faithful when Macson was in danger, and He was gracious when my mind became unraveled.

I know the darkness may descend again, but I can say with all confidence that whatever comes, I will eventually find a way to sing in the dead of night, where stars are the only markers in the sky. Because I have hope that neither life nor death, neither angels nor demons, neither the present nor the future, nor the powers of Hell, nor syndromic craniosyonstosis, nor coarctation of the aorta, nor sepsis, nor postpartum anxiety can steal.

# Chapter 42

We are in the golden years. Avery is too young to know why people are staring at her when we are in public, and she is easily satisfied with the answer that it's because she has the most beautiful eyelashes they've ever seen. And I'm not lying to her when I say that, because she truly does have the most impressive natural eyelashes I've ever seen on another human being—even when they're crinkled up behind the little pink glasses that she wears for her astigmatism.

I'm frequently asked how I'm going to handle bullying or rudeness toward Avery as she gets older, and I can tell you that I don't think much about it. Considering the ways that humans might hurt my little girl is not a subject I have the grace to discuss much yet. I don't have grace for it because that day is not yet here.

On a bulletin board hung in Avery's room is a medication sheet that lists all the diagnoses she has accumulated over the years. Things like "facial anomalies" and "trach dependent" and "heart and renal disease" came first. Others, like "sepsis" and "convulsion," came later. Sometimes it's hard to comprehend that the entire list applies to one little body because it's an overwhelming compilation of horrific suffering that my baby endured. Sometimes I feel sadness when I remember the bewildered Meg who watched the doctors add a new diagnosis to an already-devastating list.

Those papers are the physical representation of the death of dreams—dreams I had for Avery before she was born, dreams I had for our family, and dreams I had for myself. They're also a reminder of how God always supplied the right amount of grace when we needed it.

"Sepsis" almost tore my world to shreds, and yet Jesus carried us through.

"Shunt failure" partially stole my baby's sight and damaged her brain, yet Avery walks, talks, and sees.

"Vent dependent" was a hard pill to swallow, and then the Lord delivered Avery from it.

Each time a diagnosis was added to the list, I had enough grace to support Avery, and she was given the grace to survive. When I think of how to support Avery someday when people exclude her, ridicule her, and try to make her feel inferior for something that is no more a part of her identity than the color of her eyes or hair, I don't have a good answer. All I know is that wherever there is pain, there also is Jesus. To sit and think about holding my teenage daughter as she cries because of hateful words makes me feel like I might go crazy, so I don't. The only thing I can think to do is to prepare her to look to Jesus for her identity—to rest in what He says about her instead of what the world tries to tell her.

So as she grows, I'll tell her that her exterior has nothing to do with her, that physical beauty is the luck of the DNA draw. I'll tell her that no one's power comes from the way they look; it's only found in their heart, in their work ethic, and in their ability to be kind and generous with others. I'll teach her about firm boundaries. I'll tell her about how Jesus tells us to turn the other cheek when people try to hurt us. I'll remind her of all the battles she's already won, of all the things she's set her hand to do and conquered. I'll tell her that I would take anyone's hard work over their talent, their quiet bravery over their bravado. I'll teach her that age cannot dull and time cannot steal the power of a courageous heart.

One thing I've learned about dreams is to hold them with a very loose grip. Dreams are nothing more than wishes. If the dreams we have are from the Lord, then I believe He'll bring them to fruition when and how He sees fit (although in my experience, they rarely look as I anticipated). And if the dreams are not from Him, in my experience, He'll dash them to pieces like pottery until we're ready to realize the bigger plans He has for us. Either way, dreams are usually a very painful subject.

When I discovered I was pregnant with Avery, I had a host of dreams for her—or really wishes about who she should be and what her life would be like. At the time, I had them for all of my children, and I was unaware how much my "dreams" were more like illusions. Particularly the illusion that if I raised my children perfectly, I could control the outcome of their development—that if I kept them from all suffering or harm, their lives would be happy.

Becoming the parent of a medically fragile child whose future I can barely foresee more than a year or so down the road has shattered that illusion. I still have no idea how many of Avery's complications could affect her long-term quality of life. I know she has another major facial reconstructive surgery in her future, but I have no idea how that will change or improve her life. I'd like to believe it will be better as a result, but experience has taught me that I can never be certain. The only truth on to which I hold is that life will change, for better or worse, but God never will. He will always be good.

I've fumbled back and forth between having no dreams and making big plans, and I think wisdom says to find a sweet spot right in the middle. Make plans, enjoy the present, and trust that there's hope for the future, even if it looks a little different than we anticipated.

We will never parent perfectly. We were never designed to. Our children, our marriages, and our families are organically evolving organisms that will experience loss and setbacks and unforeseeable challenges. Happiness does not result from a lack of suffering; sometimes happiness results from suffering and the joy that can be found in the midst of it, from the self-trust that comes from knowing we've valiantly persevered in battle and won, and from the reminder that God sustained us when we should have perished.

I've found that holding tightly to Jesus and loosely to everything else keeps dreams from becoming idols and keeps Jesus on the throne of our lives where He belongs.

# Chapter 43

"What is the number before four, Lolly?" I asked. Not long after Ryan's first birthday, we were sitting at the kitchen table after dinner working on her kindergarten homework. Macson was home-schooling for a second year, but we had elected to send Lolly to public school. The decision had seemed huge at first, since I had never attended public school before, nor sent any of my children to public school. But this was another example of my making a big deal where there was none to be made. Our experience with Lolly's school had been nothing short of delightful.

I had made a habit out of doing things the hard way when the easier way was more sensible. When Macson had gone to school, I sent him to an expensive private Christian school. I felt that I needed to be a purist and only expose him to Christian curricula in order to protect him. I thought that paying an exorbitant amount for his education made me a more noble parent, that I needed to stretch our finances beyond their capacity to show that I really cared about my children. All wrong.

The Christian school that Macson attended was indeed lovely and provided a thorough education, but I realized that Lolly could get an equally excellent experience at our nearby public primary school. And allowing her to learn from a "secular" curriculum wouldn't ruin her forever. She could learn about Jesus and choose to follow Him if she chose, with or without an exclusively Christian education. I didn't need to make our life harder just for the sake of doing things the hard way. Sometimes the easy way is just as good.

"Ugh," Lolly responded, throwing her hands in the air. I knew she wanted to join Avery in the living room to play with their toy horses. Lolly is particularly bright and quite precocious, but she had not quite grasped the concept of "before" and "after" in relation to numbers. Give the girl a book and she can read all day, but apparently math class happens right before recess at school, and Lolly is definitely more concerned with the sand boxes and slides than with math.

"Three!" came a little voice from the living room.

Cody was clearing dishes from the table and stopped abruptly. Our eyes met and grew wide. Avery was playing with her toys while she waited for Lolly to join her in the living room, and she didn't even bother to look in our direction when she answered.

"OK, Smarty Pants, what's the number after four?" I asked, setting Lolly's paper aside for the moment. I had been homeschooling Avery, but very informally, and we had mostly been working on the alphabet and gross motor skills like drawing straight lines, circles without "tails," and cutting with scissors.

"Five," Avery said with a shrug.

Cody and I looked at each other again. Lolly tugged on my arm and said, "OK, ask me again. I've got it." She did indeed understand the math question now and only needed the motivation of competing with her little sister, but we expected that. Cody and I were stunned by all the things that Avery was able to grasp just by listening. I hadn't taught her much about math other than counting and recognizing numbers from zero to ten, and yet she was able to understand a concept beyond her preschool level.

"OK, how many letters are in the alphabet, Avery?"

"Twenty-six."

"And what are the two ways that you can write each letter?"

"Uppercase and lowercase."

"And how do you spell your name?"

"A-V-E-R-Y."

"And do you know the days of the week?"

Avery rattled them off in a sing-song voice.

Cody broke into a huge, dimpled smile. "I guess she's really getting it," he said, returning to the dishes.

She really was. We all were. We were figuring out how to thrive in a life that had forced us merely to survive for so long. We were learning how to love and support each other, all while leaning on Jesus. Everyone had told us how hard the first year with a medically fragile child would be, but no one had warned us how long it would take for us to feel normal in our new way of living. We each had to grieve the life that was bygone, the dreams we'd had, and our expectations for the future. Each member of our family had suffered and lost something, but in the economy of God, nothing is lost that will not eventually be restored.

*       *       *

Avery's doctors had warned us about her possible limitations. We knew from birth that her hearing and vision could be compromised at some point in her life. We were told that choosing her trach would severely limit her ability to speak. We were told during particularly tough hospital admissions that the damage to her brain might limit her ability to walk. The neurologists warned us that repeated seizures like the ones Avery had experienced during her first year of life would have lasting consequences that would take years to fully realize, meaning that she might suffer from cognitive deficits. We were warned that her Chiari malformation might force her to need a trach and ventilator forever.

The only thing that has been consistently true for Avery is that her vision is limited. She overcame each of the other obstacles before her fifth birthday. I don't think it's because we were special or because we did everything right. We didn't. There were things I would do differently if I could go back in time. There were times I was quiet when I should have been loud, and there were times I was loud and fearful when I should have been quiet.

I think Jesus knew what He had planned for Avery, and nothing was going to stop that. I think He was always in control. I think He only ever wanted Cody and me to be faithful, to persevere, to resolutely trust Him with our children's lives.

I think Avery's success has nothing to do with me. She and Jesus lead the way. I just need to follow.

# Chapter 44

A white box was delivered to our house. Its contents included six pink bracelets that, like these words you now read, were the manifestation of long-awaited things. The emblem on the front of each bracelet was a small circle with two smaller circles on top, one on either side.

"Avery, our bracelets are here!" I called out to her excitedly. The "MagicBands" had an image of Mickey Mouse's ears right in the middle.

In two weeks, Avery would be going to Disney World on the trip that her Poppa promised her when no one was sure she would ever leave the hospital with a soul still inhabiting her tiny body. The night that three residents had held her upright so she could repeatedly have a needle tap her spine, her Poppa had dreamt of this trip for the first time—and now it was almost time to go. For days during that season, Avery's unoccupied eyes had been fixed on nothing as her brain seized. Now those little eyes were going to see Walt Disney World behind her pink glasses, surrounded by the longest, most beautiful eyelashes on the planet.

Our entire family would be joining us on this trip. My parents and each of their eight children, their children's spouses, and all of the grandchildren (twenty-four children and counting)—forty people in all would be going on what we had affectionately called "Avery's Trip" for years. All of our MagicBands were pink because pink is Avery's favorite color. Like we had always planned, we would each wear a red shirt with the words "Avery's Trip to Disney World 2019" to the amusement park for a few days.

Her shirt would be different—it would say "I'm Avery" on the back because her journey had been special. It had been especially hard and good and harrowing and hopeful. It had been a one-in-a-million kind of journey with a one-in-a-million kind of girl, and along the way, I realized that we're all one-in-a-million kinds of people. Maybe we don't all have a rare syndrome or a tracheostomy, but we all carry unique scars, and our hearts are home to awful, beautiful, brutal stories that no one else in the world can tell.

You are the only you. I am the only me. Avery is definitely the only Avery.

✳     ✳     ✳

The weeks leading up to our trip were a whirlwind of excitement, minus the fact that we would be commencing on an extensive road trip with a gaggle of small children. I was thrilled to be going to the Happiest Place on Earth with all the people I loved the most, but if you think traveling for two days with four children—including one child with a tracheostomy and an energetic one-year-old—is easy or carefree, it was most certainly not. The trip was exhausting, but it was worth it. I have found that everything in life is like that.

I had spent most weekends in the months prior to our trip locked away in my bedroom with my laptop and a steaming cup of coffee in the hope of finishing my biggest project of the year—the book you're now reading. I would emerge for meals and a workout each afternoon, and Cody would bring Ryan to me to nurse every few hours or as needed, depending on his level of fussiness (I'll leave the "he" being fussy up to your imagination).

I took a break from working the weekend before Thanksgiving to make extensive lists and pack way too many bags. Avery's medical supplies took up most of an entire suitcase. In previous years, packing her bag for a trip so far from home would have induced severe anxiety, but now I pack with ease. What was once laborious has become second nature to me. That's the payoff of refusing to quit—most things in life get easier with time.

Macson and I made a trip to the library for several audiobooks to listen to on our drive, and I began considering what this trip symbolized for our family. I knew, no matter what happened or how exhausting it might be, that this was a once-in-a-lifetime kind of trip. It was likely one of the last big adventures my entire family would take together. It would be one for the memory books, one we talked about for the rest of our lives. It was the trip that commemorated the fact that Avery had lived when all seemed lost. It was a trip about celebrating miracles. It was a trip about celebrating Avery.

When we arrived at the amusement park, we were all awestruck. The park had been decorated for the holidays, and Walt Disney World's usual splendor was compounded by dramatic displays of sparkling light. The castle in Magic Kingdom displayed glittering ice caps, which were both breathtakingly beautiful and slightly incongruous with the eighty-degree temperatures of Florida.

Forty humans—big and small—in red shirts walked through the various check-in stations and then stepped to the right, just inside the Magic Kingdom gate, to get a picture taken of our entire group. Disney's photographer snapped picture after picture. He offered to take photos with some of our smartphones as well. We thanked him for his thoroughness, explaining the reason for the trip and why it was so important for us to commemorate it with photographs. He was obviously moved and shared with us that he had never seen a group like ours in his eleven years as a photographer at Disney.

Once we had finished our photoshoot, we headed toward Cinderella's Castle, where we stopped to watch a trolley parade. Just before starting the performance, one of the dancers read our shirts and, in the middle of the street while surrounded by a crowd, asked which one of us was Avery. Someone pointed to her. I was carrying Avery in my arms when the beautiful cast member walked right up to us, engaged Avery with questions for a moment, and then dedicated the entire performance to her. Avery was shy and a little embarrassed at being the center of attention in such a big, public way, but tears streamed down my face. I was so touched by the performer's attentiveness to her and how beautifully she and the other performers honored my baby. That gesture felt like ministry to me.

"I should not have worn mascara today!" I said, laughing and wiping black streaks from my cheeks where my tears had made my makeup run.

Everywhere we went, Disney cast members went out of their way to include Avery and lavish sweet attention on her. During a performance of *Belle's Enchanted Storytime*, the actress playing Belle singled Avery out, included her in the show, and ended the performance by enveloping her in the biggest hug. All day, she was known as "Princess Avery." I teared up a lot during the trip.

Disney's program for people with disabilities gave Avery special access to certain rides and shorter wait times to meet her favorite princesses. Every cast member we encountered accepted Avery without once drawing back, without once showing any notice of her obvious physical uniqueness.

We stayed in the park until dark. The moon hung high overhead, and the stars twinkled in the sky, mostly hidden by the glow of Disney World's lights. Avery's last ride of the day was a roller coaster. She easily met the height requirement, but because of her previous decompression surgery and the possible instability of her cervical spine, I first tested the ride with Lolly to ensure that it was suitable for Avery to experience.

The Barnstormer was Lolly's first roller coaster as well. She rode it bravely, but mentioned to Avery afterward that she had been a little scared during the twists and turns. I wasn't entirely convinced that Avery was ready for a real roller coaster, but she begged me to let her go. I decided that Cody would be the best person to take her on it because he could keep her the safest, so I kissed her cheek and sent her to enjoy her first high-speed ride. Once it was over, Cody carried her down the exit ramp and set her back in her stroller.

Avery was quiet for a moment before raising her hands in the air and saying, "Lolly, that wasn't scary AT ALL." She screamed the next sentence: "I LOVED IT!"

Our entire group roared with laughter. Not to be left out, though he could not understand what was happening, Ryan threw his head back in a baby giggle, flashing the deep dimples on both sides of his face. He had been the perfect Disney participant all day, and I couldn't help but marvel at how this child, who had once been a nightmare infant, had turned into a delightful, delicious toddler. He had been such a gift, though an admittedly hard-to-carry gift at times. He was the treasure I hadn't asked to be entrusted with, but the joy and completion that he has brought to our family has been well worth the struggle. Like Avery. Like each of my children, really.

The fireworks display signaled the end of our first day at Walt Disney World. Watching Cinderella's Castle light up with the projected images of all my favorite Disney characters throughout the years was dazzling and deeply moving. Avery and Ryan had fallen asleep in their stroller when we trekked back to the bus terminal to catch a ride back to our hotel.

I held my darling brown-haired girl in my arms as the bus sped away in the night, thinking of how this trip of a lifetime had happened because of her. Each of her family members was being blessed because she had come to the Earth, because she had fought to keep from slipping behind the veil, and because she had lived. I thought of how in all the struggle, Jesus had been with us. In the darkness and the wandering and the grief and the waiting, knowing Him better had made the journey worth taking. And He had even made all of us better along the way. I looked out the bus window, up into the dark Florida sky, and saw the stars.

*Kinda like those*, I thought. Even in the blackness, the bleakness of hardship, Jesus had lit the way with stars, souvenirs for participating in His work. Fellowship with Him in suffering. Endurance. Perseverance. Character. Hope. Purpose. Love. Trust. A story of His goodness to share with the world.

It was past midnight when I snuggled into bed and drifted off to sleep. Our first day at Walt Disney World had been perfect.

I couldn't wait to see what tomorrow would bring.